# *End*
# OF STORY?

# *End* OF STORY?

## *Stephen* TRAVIS

inter-varsity press

INTER-VARSITY PRESS
38 De Montfort Street, Leicester LE1 7GP, England

*First published 1997*
*Reprinted 1999*

British Library Cataloguing in Publication Data
A catalogue record for this book is available from the British Library.

ISBN 0-85110-889-X

Set in Garamond No. 3

Typeset in Great Britain by Parker Typesetting Service, Leicester

Printed in Great Britain by Cox & Wyman Ltd, Reading, Berkshire.

*Inter-Varsity Press is the book-publishing division of the Universities and
Colleges Christian Fellowship (formerly the Inter-Varsity Fellowship), a
student movement linking Christian Unions in universities and colleges
throughout the United Kingdom and the Republic of Ireland, and a member
movement of the International Fellowship of Evangelical Students. For
information about local and national activities write to UCCF, 38 De
Montfort Street, Leicester LE1 7GP.*

# Contents

# TOWARDS 2000

It was New Year's Eve. The streets of Rome were filled with the sound of people singing and shouting. Thousands swarmed into the city's squares, lighting up the night with torches. Above them the church bells began to toll. But this was no mere festive announcement of a new year. The year was 999, and the bells carried a terrible warning: 'I praise the true God, I call the people, I assemble the priests, I mourn the dead, I put Satan to flight and I ring in the last judgment.'

In anticipation of this momentous event, many people had reformed their lives. Stealing was rare, bakers gave away bread free of charge, enemies were reconciled and the priests worked overtime hearing confessions.

When midnight struck, the crowd fell silent, waiting for the sky to fall in, the earth to swallow them up and the End to come. Nothing happened. Slowly they stirred as if waking from a bad dream. Weeping and laughing with relief, they began to hug each other. The bells of every church began to ring with joyful confidence. 'The bitter cup has passed,' wrote one observer, 'and the world is reborn.'

Not only in Rome was the turn of the millennium anticipated with such excitement. In September 999 a bright meteor stirred alarm and expectation among many in England who saw it. French nuns saw 'fiery armies fighting in the sky'. In Antwerp, Tanchelm persuaded his followers that he was the Messiah reborn and declared that the end of the world was near. He distributed his bathwater to the faithful, who drank it as if it were the wine of the holy communion.

All over Europe – threatened as it was by nomadic horsemen from Asia, Saracens plundering Italian villages and Norsemen invading the British Isles – there were people convinced that the dawn of the year 1000 would be the evening of the world. And in Jerusalem thousands of pilgrims in a state of hysteria flocked to the place where they expected Christ to descend from the clouds.

## The edge of a new millennium

Now, for only the second time in Christian history, we stand on the edge of a new millennium. And the prophets of both doom and hope are out in force. I knew something was up when I read the advert on the side of a bus: 'Disney's *Snow White and the Seven Dwarfs* – at the cinema for the last time this century.' So we really *are* approaching a climactic moment of history!

Of course, there's nothing particularly special about years like 1000 and 2000. Yet we find such round numbers both convenient and fascinating. There was nothing really different about, say, the years 1959 and 1961. But we speak about 'the swinging sixties' as though a whole new era suddenly dawned when the calendar fell open at January 1960. And nothing will persuade us that really big round numbers aren't loaded with extra significance.

So the year 2000 becomes the object of increasing fascination. Books appear with titles like *Planet Earth 2000 AD: Will Mankind Survive?* And juggling with biblical numbers becomes a growth industry. At the last count there were sixty-five TV stations and 922 radio stations in the United States devoted to end-of-the-world news and features. In 1992 televangelist Jack Van Impe predicted: 'I believe the President of the USA during the next eight years may face horrendous decisions concerning World War III and even Armageddon.' And in his book *Armageddon*, Grant R. Jeffrey announced that the year 2000 'is a probable termination date for the last days'.

## Seeing into the future

But prophecies focused on the end of the twentieth century are no new phenomenon. Nostradamus, a sixteenth-century French doctor who turned to mysticism and prophecy, expressed his predictions in four-line poems. Though many of them are so ambiguous that you can make them mean anything you like, others seem to refer quite precisely to specific events. One passage points specifically to the end of the century:

> In 1999 and seven months,
> from the sky will come a great kind of terror.
> He will bring to life the great king of the Mongols.
> Before and after, war reigns heavily.
> (Century 10, quatrain 72)

Nostradamus glimpses a period of global conflict. But it is not, for him, the end of history. He speaks also of a period of peace lying beyond the war. And his remaining prophecies cover a further thousand years or more.

Why is there such widespread interest in prophecies, whether they come from medieval mystics or from masters of media communications? Such prophets offer salvation from uncertainty. They proclaim to a confused and fearful world: 'Everything is under control. If you listen to my prophecy you will be safe. You will be on the side of God and his purpose.' Even prophecies of chaos and disaster bring reassurance if you are persuaded that they come as no surprise, but were foreseen long ago.

And reassurance is in short supply, especially in the western world. Bishop Lesslie Newbigin returned to England in 1974 after working in India for nearly forty years. He was often asked what his greatest difficulty was in moving back into British life. He always replied: 'The disappearance of hope.' Somehow even in the slums of Madras there was always the feeling that things could be improved. But in Britain confidence had given way to cynicism. According to a 1994 survey of young people in various countries, only one third of British fifteen-year-olds thought the world would be a better place in the year 2000, compared with two-thirds in the developing world.

We face a crisis of hope both in our personal lives and in the world as a whole. Let's look at some of the reasons.

## Destruction of the environment

On 15 February 1996 the 147,000-ton tanker *Sea Empress* was carrying her cargo towards the oil refinery in Milford Haven, South Wales. Although a pilot was on board to guide her into the harbour, she ran aground on rocks which lay hidden below the waves. Before salvage was under way she had spilled 70,000 tons of crude oil, devastating hundreds of miles of coastline, killing thousands of sea birds and ruining a fishing industry. The technology and the experience to see her safely to her destination were available, but a combination of bad weather and bad judgment ensured that the disaster happened.

The world approaching a new millennium is on a similarly hazardous course. The only certainty is an unstable future. Every day we are confronted by new evidence of a world heading for collision. We don't know how to stop it and we don't trust anyone who claims to be in charge.

The *Sea Empress* story simply illustrates what is happening all the time as human beings abuse the fragile balance of nature. Every year twenty million acres of virgin rainforest in Africa, Asia and Latin America are burned, destroying for ever plant and animal species and the traditional homes of native peoples. Since 1945 half of the world's rainforests – the 'lungs' of all living beings – have been destroyed. If rainforests continue to be wiped out at the present rate, they will disappear by 2050 – making thousands of animal and plant species extinct, turning fruitful land into desert, and drastically reducing the earth's capacity to produce the oxygen on which our lives depend.

The explosion at the Chernobyl power station in 1986 spread nuclear pollution from Ukraine to Scotland and beyond, leaving an increasing incidence of cancer in its wake. In Ogoniland, Nigeria, thirty years' collaboration between Shell and the Nigerian government left farmland squelching with oil from leaked pipes and the local people with no financial or social benefit from the fouling of their land.

The ever-increasing use of fossil fuels in industry, cars and homes pumps poison into the air we breathe. The resulting carbon dioxide produces 'global warming', which seems already to be affecting average temperatures around the world. Polar ice is melting and will lead to higher sea levels and the flooding of low-lying land. Some once-fertile plains may become deserts. J. C. W. White of the Institute of Arctic and Alpine Research at the University of Colorado commented: 'If the earth had an operating manual, the chapter on climate might begin with a warning that the system has been adjusted at the factory for optimum comfort – so don't touch the dials.' But we have been fiddling with the knobs for decades.

Our release of CFCs and other gases into the atmosphere has created holes in the ozone layer, allowing through more of the sun's harmful ultraviolet rays. British government advisers reported in 1996 that these rays will cause a 10% increase in the number of today's children who will develop skin cancer in later life. Although steps are now being taken to curb these chemicals, it will be about 2010 before the protective ozone layer begins to repair itself. The increase in ultraviolet rays also interferes with the genetic structure of plants and animals. This may lead to crop failure and disrupt the growth of creatures in the oceans.

With our plastic packaging and metal drink-cans, we are a throwaway society. But the truth is that there is no 'away' to throw anything. We are just piling it up at our own back door. Already in 1988 *National Geographic*'s editor was writing: 'Environmental apocalypse is now. We've borrowed the earth from our children and unless we come around very quickly, we are going to give it back to them in very bad shape.'

'The world is dying and nobody can stop it,' comments a character at the climax of Ben Elton's novel *This Other Eden*. 'It's always been dying, ever since man began to take from it more than he needed. *This planet is a finite quantity, logic dictates that it cannot be consumed indefinitely* . . . Earth as we know it is finished, because man rules it and man is incapable of acting responsibly! Of thinking in anything other than the short term.'

# Population growth

The rapid growth of the population is another challenge confronting us. It took 2 million years for the human population of the world to reach 1 billion in about 1830. By 1930 it had doubled to 2 billion. Around 8% of all the human beings who have ever lived are alive today. By the year 2000 we shall share the earth with 6.2 billion people, and the number will rise to beyond 10 billion before it levels off during the next century.

It is wrong to talk of population growth as a problem, as though children are to be blamed for being born. A child in India with seven sisters and three brothers is not less valuable than a child in Britain or North America with only one sister. In poorer countries population growth is a symptom rather than a problem. People with uncertain healthcare and no pension have children to provide security in their old age. And a family in India or Malawi uses far less of the earth's resources than a family in the developed world. So who is the problem – us or them?

With growth on this scale we are moving into uncharted territory. We simply don't know how many of us the planet can feed. What we do know is the basic biological fact that any creature which becomes so numerous that its food supply cannot sustain it is bound to crash. Already in the last fifty years over-fishing has brought very serious decline in fish stocks in the seas around Europe and North and South America. According to the United Nations Food and Agriculture Organization, thirteen of the world's fifteen great fishing-grounds are in serious decline. Crises of this kind are set to multiply.

## Inequalities of wealth

The gap between rich and poor nations is increased by these population pressures. For when populations grow, any economic improvement is swallowed up in providing for the new people. But that is not the only problem they face. Many poor countries owe huge sums of money to rich countries. For every £1 given in aid to the Two-Thirds World, £3 is paid back through interest on debts.

Year after year they repay millions – with no hope of ever discharging the debt. Each year Uganda spends $3 a head on health and $17 on debt repayment, while one in five of its children dies from diseases which could be prevented by basic healthcare. Brazil is one of the world's biggest food exporters. Yet each year 400,000 Brazilian children die from hunger-related illnesses. Food sold to rich nations brings in money to repay the debt to rich nations. And the children go hungry. 'If the Amazon is the lungs of the world,' said a Brazilian trade unionist, 'then the debt is its pneumonia.'

Debt on this scale brings despair. It leads to instability and violence. One of many causes of the terrible conflict in Rwanda in 1994–5 was the hardship caused by the debt problem, which widened the inequalities between the 'haves' and the 'have-nots' within the country.

## Arms out of control

Violence is an increasing threat around the world. Modern warfare means that more people – over 100 million – have been killed in war since 1900 than in the whole previous history of human conflict. World powers spend $2 million a minute on research and manufacture of weapons. Much of what they make is sold to developing countries, often to governments who will use them to oppress their own people. Indonesia uses British arms to suppress dissent in East Timor. The Nigerian government, well known for its human-rights abuses, is another major customer.

For comfortable westerners, violence is no longer at a safe distance. In many cities, fatal shootings, driven by gang warfare and the trade in illegal drugs, are a daily occurrence. The growing gap between rich and poor goes hand in hand with an increasing partnership of robbery and violence. A US security-industry executive offered this grim forecast about the twenty-first century: 'A world where one third of the population protects a second third from the other third.'

## Transnational companies rule the world

Another feature of our world in summed up in the word *globalization*. No part of the world is safe from the influence of decisions and events elsewhere. Some 70% of world trade is controlled by transnational corporations – huge companies which are often wealthier than the countries in which they operate. Shell, for example, has annual sales of $100 billion – three times the annual income of Nigeria's 100 million people.

With such economic power, they can often write the rules by which business operates. They switch production to countries with the lowest wages – and move on a few years later when conditions elsewhere are more favourable for profit-making. They transfer assets so as to show profits in the country with the lowest taxes. Some companies sell medicines and pesticides in the Two-Thirds World which have been banned in developed countries because of their harmful effects on people and the environment. This is good for shareholders, but not so good for many of the countries where they operate.

Anywhere in the world you can buy a Toyota car, a Bic pen or a can of Coke, or you can see *Baywatch* or *The X Files* on TV. To a westerner used to such products, this may seem no bad thing, until you look at it through another culture's eyes. In 1992 a remote African village got electricity for the first time. Within two weeks the people bought a TV and video and village life was wrecked overnight. They were up until the small hours watching Sylvester Stallone, dragged in an instant from traditional culture into a sophisticated and violent western world.

## Changing attitudes

Alongside such globalization has come a growth of individualism. Perhaps because we feel driven by worldwide forces too big for us to control, we want above all else to 'express ourselves' and to 'fulfil ourselves'. We justify our actions by saying, 'I have a duty to myself.' We seek success through popularity with friends, through making money and through keeping up with the trendsetters. We refuse to be bullied into accepting the rules set by a previous generation. Life is about being myself, not a photocopy of someone else. 'I can make it on my own. I don't need other people, and other people will have to manage without me.'

Those who feel like this may, of course, have little interest in the big issues I have just described. 'If I am to fulfil myself,' they may say, 'I can do without being disturbed by global issues which I can't change anyway.' But we can't separate ourselves from the rest of the world quite so easily.

The focus on self is strengthened by the feeling that our leaders have failed us. Who would have guessed twenty years ago that today the institutions on which our society has been built would be so widely questioned? The police and the justice system have been weakened by scandal and the abuse of power. The image of the British Royal Family is tarnished, perhaps fatally. The church is regarded by many as irrelevant to life in the real world. Governments are seen as paralysed by narrow party interest and incapable of making long-term change for the benefit of all.

So the people who are strongly committed to change turn less to politics and more to single-issue pressure groups. They campaign for animal rights or gay rights or disability rights. They are against road-building or censorship or the manufacture of landmines. Such passionate concentration on specific issues offers hopes of real change. But maybe it also locks us into an intolerable *Catch 22* situation. Our individualism makes us distrust government, so we abandon politics in favour of single-issue campaigning. But we find ourselves competing against rival pressure groups with different goals. And that removes us even further from any hope of finding a just future for all.

Of course, the picture isn't all bleak. There is so much in the world which brings joy and freedom and colour and excitement. There is progress as well as calamity. Every day something happens about which we can say, 'That makes life worth living.' Yet we know that the world is not as it should be. We need a new vision, a new way of looking at the world and at ourselves.

# FACING THE FUTURE

---

Confronted by these glimpses of where the world is going, how are we to react? Among the people I meet I find a range of attitudes towards the future.

## Good times ahead?

Some are confidently optimistic. Helen, in her twenties, expects to fulfil her potential in life. She isn't impressed by politicians, but sees them as largely irrelevant to progress. She has good prospects in her job and enjoys the responsibility it offers. The world is at her feet. There will be time later for more serious relationships and, maybe, children.

For others there is an optimism based on the ability of technology to solve problems. Some people have a touching faith in technology – like the woman in London who called an engineer to repair her fax machine. When asked what was wrong, she replied, 'My daughter's on holiday in Spain and she left her bikini behind. She phoned me to send it to her but it wouldn't go through the fax.'

In 1905, T. Baron Russell wrote *A Hundred Years Hence: The Expectations of an Optimist*, in which he predicted newspapers with colour photos, high-quality sound recordings and sound films, and the invention of the videophone (which he called the 'teleautoscope'). He foresaw that there would be bigger and bigger shops, cutting out the middleman, and that trains would run at 200 mph.

But he was less successful in his predictions of moral progress. He argued that by the end of the twentieth century, humanity would learn not to waste limited natural resources. And he believed that war would become a thing of the past. People would become so appalled at the destructive power of modern weapons and the financial cost of fighting wars that they would cease to allow governments to declare wars and to send armies to fight them.

Similar misjudgments litter the writings of more recent futurologists. In *Megatrends 2000* John Naisbitt and Patricia Aburdene radiate an optimism based on confidence in the marketplace to deliver the goods, on technology to solve problems, and on the human drive for a better life. They hardly mention the obstacles which might cloud their vision, managing only one page, for example, on environmental issues.

In the 1970s, Hermann Kahn suggested that in a hundred years' time we could expect a world population of 15 billion, with each family owning three houses, two cars and perhaps a submarine. He admitted that probably seventy major world problems would crop up even before the twentieth century was finished, but 'given moderately reasonable behaviour', the human race would survive to enjoy his promised utopia.

With optimists like that, who needs pessimists? What confidence do history and our own experience give us that humanity can face scores of major problems and approach each one reasonably? The fact that dictionaries in their recent editions have added phrases like 'ethnic cleansing', 'date rape' and 'road rage' is not exactly reassuring.

Feeling unable to share such confidence about the future, others turn to escapism. For, as T. S. Eliot said, 'mankind cannot bear too much reality'. Some escape to the past. They return to the secure world of antique furniture, *Sound of Music* videos and unchanging churches.

Others escape into entertainment which takes their minds off the harsh realities of life. The fact that Las Vegas is the fastest-growing city in the United States somehow symbolizes this craving for amusement which diverts us from the real world. Not that there's anything bad about entertainment in itself, of course. But an excess of it becomes a drug which makes us numb to the world outside and to the emptiness inside us.

Yet even though I may escape for the weekend from the pressures of work or the bleakness of life, I cannot escape from myself. So perhaps pessimism is a more realistic option? Whatever the futurologists and the politicians tell us, many of us are more anxious than optimistic about the future. And to worry about the future of the planet seems a luxury to those whose own situation is insecure. For every young person confident about his or her prospects, there is another worried about finding a job.

## The world isn't working

A cartoon in the *New Yorker* showed a shop assistant saying to a customer: 'Now, Madam, this toy is ideally suited to teach your child to live in the modern world — whichever way you try to put it together, it doesn't fit.'

That sense of a world not fitting together isn't just an

observation of how the world is 'out there'. It goes deep inside us. Whereas previous generations had assumed that they could change things, today's young people feel powerless and undervalued. In a climate of individualism, they find not self-fulfilment but loneliness. In an age when computers are starting to talk to us, they find their neighbours becoming more remote. In a world of virtual reality, they lose the real world of people with whom they can share their deepest feelings.

In 1994, Kurt Cobain, lead singer with the band Nirvana, killed himself. His songs expressed the emptiness and confusion that many of his fans experienced. According to Steve Ayers, months later the music press was still getting letters from grieving fans. 'I'm crying . . . My sweet Kurt is dead . . . I have attempted suicide twice . . . Sometimes I really want to die . . . Inside my head, I'm dead, with Kurt.' Not just a handful of letters, but enough to prompt a journalist to start a support group for those who sent them.

This is an emptiness which cannot be filled by Ecstasy and all-night parties. It is the emptiness of people who deeply distrust 'solutions' thrust on them by others. They feel lied to by the media and by politicians. Many feel let down by parents whose relationship has broken down or whose obsession with material goals has starved their spirits. For role models they have only people like Bono of U2, who said: 'How can you be spokesman of a generation if you've nothing to say other than "Help"?'

## Signs of hope

This is no mere cynicism. It is a searching despair which carries within it the seeds of hope. In the title of his best-selling first novel *Generation X*, Douglas Coupland coined the phrase which identifies the twenty-somethings of today. He portrayed this generation's feelings of emptiness, worthlessness and lack of hope.

In his third novel, *Life After God*, he probes more deeply below the surface. Confronting issues such as ecological disaster, marriage break-up, loneliness and death, he explores 'the unique sorrow of being human'. Having your senses dulled by a world of MTV, junk food and shopping malls, he says, leads to 'believing in nothing'.

My secret is that I need God – that I am sick and can no longer make it alone. I need God to help me give, because I no longer seem capable of giving; to help me be kind, as I no longer seem capable of kindness; to help me love, as I seem beyond being able to love.

This *searching for a new power to live by* suggests that we are not made merely for MTV and shopping malls. There's more to life than BMWs or low-paid jobs. The search is a sign of hope. We search because God has made us for more than material things and short-term pleasures. 'I can no longer make it alone,' says Coupland. But maybe I was never meant to.

Another sign of hope is our *longing for justice*. From the child's first cry of 'It's not fair!' there is built into us a sense of what is just. When we see the system stacked against the weak and vulnerable, we may be too lazy to do much about it. But we know it's not right. We are reaching out for a different kind of world.

A third sign of hope is our *longing for community*. Most of us are frightened by the brutal competitiveness in society, which drives the weak to the wall and increases the gap between rich and poor. We protect ourselves from those who have let us down – maybe parents, or politicians, or lovers – by trying to survive on our own. And in loneliness we crave for community, for relationships which last, for a world where people can be trusted. We look for a society where people are turned towards each other for support rather than against each other in conflict. We don't know how it will come, but we won't give up the dream.

Another sign is the welling up of *wonder and hope* which parents feel at the birth of a child. Even the most cynical and world-weary father is overcome by a sense of humble amazement as he holds the tiny, vulnerable baby in his arms. For the first time in years he can believe that a new beginning can happen. For the sake of his child he wants the world to be a safer and more wholesome place. He catches a vision of the world as it is meant to be.

A final sign of hope is the *search for patterns* in our lives. Surrounded by apparently chance happenings, we look for meaning, for patterns that make sense of life. Novels or fairy stories with happy endings are one way in which we feed our hope that there is meaning in life's ups and downs. When we look back on periods of life, we try to see how different bits fit together, and how the changes and developments were 'meant'. We feel that if there is no pattern, life has no point. It's just 'a tale told by an idiot, full of sound and fury, signifying nothing'.

The big question is this. If we find these longings inside us, where do they come from? Are they just wishful thinking, strategies we adopt to stop ourselves going mad? Or do they point to the way things are meant to be? Might they be our Creator's hints that there is hope for us and for the world, if only we could follow the clues?

# 'Everything is meaningless'

One person searching for clues was the Old Testament writer of Ecclesiastes, 'the Philosopher' ('the Teacher', NIV). He was a man looking for meaning. Like the French writer Albert Camus, he believed that the most important question facing us all is 'to decide whether life deserves to be lived or not'.

In his book he tells how he has pursued education, pleasure, money, power. He has immersed himself in hard work. He knows that all these things have value. But they offer no final answers. There are parts of him these things can't reach. 'Meaningless! Meaningless!' he says, 'Everything is meaningless' (Ecclesiastes 1:2).

This word 'meaningless', in the Hebrew original, speaks of a vapour, a puff of wind. And why does he write that depressing slogan across the whole of life? Because human evil, uncertainty and, above all, death cast their shadow across every search for meaning. To everyone alike, death comes like the tide that destroys the sandcastle and makes it as though it never existed. 'No-one has power over the day of his death' (Ecclesiastes 8:8).

The Philosopher is human like ourselves. He knows how to enjoy life. Yet he is haunted by questions. The uncertainties and injustices of life touch him deeply. He challenges the easy-going faith of his contemporaries. He longs to glimpse the future, but has discovered that God keeps the future to himself. We 'cannot find out what God has done from the beginning to the end' (Ecclesiastes 3:11, NRSV).

And yet he belonged to a race, the Jews, who believed that God was leading them on a journey towards a new future. Many people today can only ask, 'What do I do until the undertaker comes?' The Philosopher – at least in his more positive moments – could ask, 'What do I do until the

Messiah comes?' Even though God was hidden, there was still hope that he would make himself known in a new way. Then a whole new world would open up. We shall come back to this story in the next chapter. But first we explore the raw materials of hope.

## Hope squeezed out

'Despair assails Palestinians trapped in a gilded cage', said a headline in the *Independent* on 9 December 1995. Khamis Khodr and Mohamed al-Gulani had spent nearly eight months in the United Nations headquarters in Naqqoura, southern Lebanon. They were trapped between the Israelis, who had deported them, and the Lebanese, who had refused to receive them. In their refuge, thanks to a humanitarian worker, they had food, beds, books, television, the use of a phone, friends among the UN soldiers and £150 each a month. They watched videos and played football and chess with their UN protectors. But they had no passport, no country and no home. Neither Israel nor Lebanon would let them pass through on their way to another country. They are 'political ghosts', said one of their UN protectors. 'My life is over,' said Mr Khodr.

Cut off from both the past and the future, they were without hope. We cannot have hope without a sense of both past and future. If our future is closed in, we become desperate. In the region where I live, the rate of suicide among young people has nearly doubled in ten years. Poor job prospects, the pressure to get good exam results and the expectations of parents have combined to make more and more young people feel that the future cannot be faced.

# Looking for roots

It seems obvious that to have hope we need to have a way into the future. But we also need a link to our past. Most people who grow up as orphans or as adopted children have a deep need, sooner or later, to discover their parents. They want to know about their background and, if possible, to meet the people who gave them birth. Without a past they feel they are non-persons, and they can find no way of facing the future with hope.

In Mick Inkpen's children's book *Nothing*, a child's plaything lay forgotten in the attic. So long had it been there that even its own name was lost. The family were rummaging through the junk as they prepared to move house. 'Oh, it's nothing,' said one, as they left behind the tattered old doll.

'So that's my name,' thought the little thing. 'Nothing!'

Creeping out through a gap in the eaves, it met a cat named Toby, who announced that it had just moved house and invited Nothing to come and see. Reaching the house, it dropped Nothing into Grandpa's lap. There was a glimmer of recognition in both their faces. Grandpa pulled out an old photo album and found a fading photo of a baby, a cat and a little cuddly cloth cat made to look like the real cat.

'That's me!' said Grandpa. 'And that's Toby's great-great-great-grandfather. And this is Little Toby!'

So at last Nothing remembered who he was. Though he had lost his ears, his whiskers, his tail and his stripes, he was not Nothing, but a cloth tabby cat called Little Toby. And with the help of a good wash, and some scraps of material and thread, he became Little Toby again and was restored to his place in the family.

To have hope for the future, I need to know who I am. To know who I am, I need to know where I've come from, and to discover that I am loved and accepted as I am. I need a link with both past and future, a sense that I am on a journey towards a goal.

## 'Hoping for' and 'hoping in'

But something else is needed if we are to grasp the significance of hope. There is a difference between 'hoping for' and 'hoping in'. I may hope for many things – a secure job, a win on the Lottery, a fast car, a happy marriage, success in a football match. I may focus all my energies on achieving them. All my ambition is bound up in them. If they don't happen, I am devastated.

And if they do happen, I may find myself wondering whether they are all they were cracked up to be. Buzz Aldrin was the second man to walk on the moon. In the year following his *Apollo 11* mission he suffered from depression. In his book *Return to Earth* he described how he had spent most of his life competing for difficult goals. Now with his moon walk – 'the most important goal of all' – behind him, he suffered from 'the melancholy of all things done'. There was nowhere further to go.

But to 'hope in' someone brings a deeper perspective. A child hopes for a mountain bike for Christmas, and is disappointed to discover that his parents can't afford to buy one. But his hope and trust in his parents go deeper than his longing for the bike, and he can cope with the disappointment. Irene hopes for a cure for her cancer. Even though it doesn't come, she doesn't give in to despair because she has learnt to have confidence in God, who will never let her go. Like the ancient psalm-writer, she knows how brief life is, and that everyone's life is a mere breath. But she prays: 'Now, Lord, what do I look for? My hope is in you' (Psalm 39:5–7).

Her sense of being held by God's love transforms her future.

Chief Rabbi Jonathan Sacks was reflecting on his first visit to Auschwitz, where more than a million Jews were murdered by the Nazis. Fifty years on, he sees the Jews as a people who have walked through the valley of the shadow of death and are reaffirming life and hope.

If you come from a religious tradition that is almost 4,000 years old, much of whose history has been written in tears, and which has never given up hope . . . that does give you a very long perspective indeed . . . We have always seen that despair is premature in the human situation.

That isn't merely hope for something better to turn up. It's hope in a God who, despite the best efforts of humanity to destroy everything of value, will not give up on the people he loves.

# GOD'S MISSION STATEMENT

Every half-decent company has one. It's a crisp summary of the company's reason for existence, the goals against which it measures all its activities. The BBC, for example, describes its mission as

- providing the comprehensive, in-depth and impartial news and information coverage across a range of broadcasting outlets that is needed to support a fair and informed national debate;
- supporting and stimulating the development and expression of British culture and entertainment;
- guaranteeing the provision of programming and services that create opportunities for education;
- stimulating the communication of cultures and ideas between Britain and abroad.

Perhaps 'crisp' isn't the best way to describe this collection of rather long words. But it summarizes what the BBC is there for – its mission in life. Reading it made me wonder: does God have a mission statement?

Maybe we find it best summarized in some words of the apostle Paul: 'God's plan . . . is to bring all creation together, everything in heaven and on earth, with Christ as head' (Ephesians 1:10, GNB).

There is hope for the world because there is a God who had a plan at the beginning and will see it through to the end. It is a plan not for a fortunate few, but for the whole of his creation. And at the centre of his plan is Jesus of Nazareth – the man whose birth passed unnoticed by the news correspondents of the day, and yet was so significant that we date our history from it.

## God's track record

God's mission statement isn't simply a slogan dreamt up by the marketing people. It's the promise of a God with a track record of reaching out to a broken world. Alongside the individual stories of countless men and women who have walked briefly on this planet, there is an overarching story of God's involvement with the world. The Bible presents it as a movement from creation to completion, from beginning to end.

The Jewish people knew that the present wasn't all-important. Their life was rooted in the past – in God's loving creation of the world and particularly in their own calling to be a special people through whom the whole world would find its way to God. And it was facing towards the future, to God's promised new world where he would make all things right. So, however dark the present might be, they knew it would not be like that for ever.

Right through their history they sensed that they had a purpose to fulfil, a vision which had first been given by God to their ancestor Abraham:

I will make you into a great nation
  and I will bless you;
I will make your name great,
  and you will be a blessing.
I will bless those who bless you,
  and whoever curses you I will curse;
and all peoples on earth
  will be blessed through you.

(Genesis 12:2–3)

But through the centuries they learnt much about God which no-one can learn except through experience of life.

## False hopes and real hope

They found, for example, that real hope for the future can be found only if false hopes are dashed. There were times in Israel's history when the people got sidetracked from their journey with God. There was a time, for example, when they treated the temple in Jerusalem like a lucky charm that would protect them from disaster however much they strayed from God's way. And God sent leaders and prophets to explode such false hopes and set them again on a true path:

Do not trust in deceptive words and say, 'This is the temple of the LORD, the temple of the LORD, the temple of the LORD!' If you really change your ways and your actions and deal with each other justly, if you do not oppress the alien, the fatherless or the widow and do not shed innocent blood in this place, and if you do not follow other gods to your own harm, then I will let you live in this place, in the land I gave to your ancestors for ever and ever . . .           (Jeremiah 7:4–7)

But the Hebrew prophets not only confronted false hopes. They offered real hope with their vision of God's goals:

- to create a community of people from all nations who would live under his just and gentle rule;
- to banish the evil inside us and around us, which constantly makes human life less than it was meant to be;
- to create a world of justice where the poor are oppressed no longer;
- to build a world of peace between nations;
- to bring men and women into harmony rather than conflict with the natural world;
- to create a permanent celebration of life as all God's people experience the closeness of relationship to the living God.

This vision is scattered throughout the books of the prophets. But the flavour of it is found, for example, in Isaiah:

> Many peoples will come and say,
> 'Come, let us go up to the mountain of the LORD,
>   to the house of the God of Jacob.
> He will teach us his ways,
>   so that we may walk in his paths.'
> The law will go out from Zion,
>   the word of the LORD from Jerusalem.
> He will judge between the nations
>   and will settle disputes for many peoples.
> They will beat their swords into ploughshares
>   and their spears into pruning hooks.
> Nation will not take up sword against nation,
>   nor will they train for war any more.
>
> (Isaiah 2:3–4)

# The reign of God

If you'd asked the prophets to sum up in a phrase what they were looking forward to, they would have replied: 'We're looking for God's reign – the time when God is really King.' They had seen enough of earthly rulers who were incompetent or unjust. They had seen the evil in human hearts which no earthly ruler could control. The promise that God would be King spelt liberation and hope.

The people of Israel learnt also that God adjusts his plans to take account of human weakness. He doesn't play power-games with people. He doesn't behave like the spoilt child who says, 'If you won't play my way, I'm taking my ball home.' He allows even our failures to become part of his grand plan.

In the early days of Israel's life in the Promised Land, people expressed a longing to be ruled by a king 'like all the other nations'. The prophet Samuel saw this desire as a rejection of *God's* rule over them. When he reported it to God, God's answer was surprising. 'A king', he seemed to say, 'is a bad idea. But let them have one anyway' (1 Samuel 8).

God has a habit of not being defeated by human wrong-doing or stupidity. When we take a wrong turning, we aren't condemned to a lifetime of second best. God doesn't write us off and exclude us from his plans, or force his own way upon us simply because he knows best. Like a sympathetic friend, he comes alongside us and finds a way of working out his plan by another way. He could let the people have kings – with all the disadvantages as well as advantages this would bring – and achieve his goals through them. After all, the second of these kings would be David, and from his family the Messiah would one day be born.

The Old Testament story is an unfinished one. It's the story of hope waiting for its fulfilment, longing for the time when God will act and expecting the Messiah through whom his new world will come.

## Village drama

Come with me now to a village in the hills of Galilee. It is Saturday, and the synagogue service is about to begin. A carpenter slips in among the worshippers, as he has done here in Nazareth since boyhood. Old men grunt, and women nudge each other as he takes his place. For this young man has begun another line of business lately, and they wonder what his presence here may bring.

The time comes for the Bible to be read, and Jesus is invited to take the scroll. He reads from the prophet Isaiah a passage which speaks to Jews of how God will bring new hope to his people:

> The Spirit of the Lord is on me,
>> because he has anointed me
>> to preach good news to the poor.
> He has sent me to proclaim freedom for the prisoners
>> and recovery of sight for the blind,
> to release the oppressed,
>> to proclaim the year of the Lord's favour.

Jesus hands the scroll back to the attendant and sits down. He feels the gaze of every eye fixed intently on him. 'Today', he says, 'this scripture is fulfilled in your hearing' (see Luke 4:14–21).

It is one of the most dramatic scenes in the New Testament. And it sums up the whole meaning of Jesus' coming. It is, if you like, his mission statement. He is announcing that the old prophetic promises are now reaching their decisive fulfilment.

Jesus comes as Messiah, 'anointed' or filled with God's Spirit to declare good news to the poor and announce the dawning of God's liberation from every kind of captivity. What God's people have longed for through the centuries has arrived! The revolution of God is here. In Jesus, God has come close to his people.

## Signs of God's reign

Jesus was a preacher who commanded attention with his vivid stories, his humour, his fearless challenge to people in power, and his knack of getting straight to the heart of an issue. But he was never just a clever talker. His teaching of the truth about God and his acting in the power of God went perfectly together.

Jesus pointed to his healing miracles and his exorcisms as signs that the power of God's reign was now at work in a new way. When John the Baptist sent messengers from his prison cell to ask if Jesus really was God's chosen liberator, Jesus replied:

> Go back and report to John what you hear and see: The blind receive sight, the lame walk, those who have leprosy are cured, the deaf hear, the dead are raised, and the good news is preached to the poor. (Matthew 11:4–5)

> If I drive out demons by the Spirit of God, then the kingdom [that is, the reign] of God has come upon you. (Matthew 12:28)

All kinds of people could bear witness to this. A deranged man, tormented by evil forces within him, was made whole by

Jesus. The twelve-year-old daughter of a synagogue leader was brought back to life from her deathbed. The blind, the paralysed, the deaf and dumb were restored to full health.

No doubt there was excitement and celebration as each of these people realized the full impact of what Jesus had done for them. A man blind from birth could feast for the first time on the colour of God's creation. A woman whose illness had made her an outcast from society could take her place again among her neighbours. A child could run and laugh and play.

But these miracles were not only acts of concern for particular individuals. They were signs of what God's reign is like, and what in the end it will mean for all people. God's reign is about wholeness of life. It's about evil defeated in all its forms, life triumphing over death. It's about a society which is inclusive of all kinds of people and where no-one is consigned to the scrap-heap.

## The reign of a Father

How did Jesus describe God's reign? He said it's the reign of a Father. He taught his followers to pray, 'Our Father, may your kingdom [reign] come . . .' (Matthew 6:9). God's reign isn't the reign of a distant ruler who may never come near you in your whole life. It's the guidance of a parent who is always concerned for your well-being and loves each one as though there were no-one else to love.

Of course, some people have problems with thinking about God as Father. 'Father' is for them a negative picture because they have been abused or neglected by their own father. But when Jesus speaks in this way he isn't saying that God is just like your earthly father. He means that God has all the qualities which you could wish for in a perfect father. He understands you. He is caring, strong, gentle, always reliable. He doesn't crowd your own space but allows you to develop as a unique person. He enjoys your company.

## God's reign brings forgiveness

Jesus showed how God's reign brings forgiveness. Zacchaeus collected taxes on behalf of the Roman authorities. He was rich – and despised by his fellow Jews because he worked with the hated Romans. When Jesus came to Jericho he surprised Zacchaeus by insisting on visiting his home. Zacchaeus promised to give half his possessions to the poor and to pay back four times over any money he had gained by cheating. This showed that 'salvation has come to this house,' said Jesus (see Luke 19:1–10). The reign of God means forgiveness for past wrongs and a new beginning for the future. And when the generosity of God touches people, they become generous too.

Jesus' eating with Zacchaeus was a powerful expression of forgiveness. In the East, to share a meal had deep significance. It wasn't like sitting at the same table in McDonald's and then moving on unchanged by each other's presence. To eat with someone was to say, 'You are my brother, my sister. I accept and honour you. Whatever wrongs we may have done each other in the past, we are now committed to each other in friendship.'

Many of Jesus' best-known stories convey this news of God's forgiveness. God is like a king who wrote off the debt of a servant, even though he owed him millions of pounds (Matthew 18:23–35). He joyfully welcomes anyone who comes to him for forgiveness, as a woman rejoices when she finds her lost coin, or a shepherd his sheep, or a father his son (Luke 15).

# God's reign is for all people

Religion has a habit of setting boundaries to keep people safe and respectable, and to keep out people who don't conform to its rules. Religious leaders of Jesus' day kept out those whom they labelled as 'sinners'. They made it virtually impossible for them to change their ways and become acceptable again.

But Jesus declared that no-one was beyond the scope of God's love. 'The least, the last and the lost' were special objects of God's care. At the beginning of his ministry he included among his disciples a tax-collector and a political revolutionary – men at opposite ends of the political spectrum, equal objects of suspicion for their extreme positions. At the end he responded to the pleas of the bandit on the cross: 'Today you will be with me in paradise' (Luke 23:43).

It wasn't only the outsiders of Israel who came within the scope of God's reign. Jesus brought good news to a Samaritan woman, whose race was regarded by Jews as impure (John 4). When urged by a Roman centurion to heal his sick servant, he exclaimed, 'I have not found such great faith even in Israel' (Luke 7:9). The old barriers were being broken down. The promise to Abraham was at last beginning to come true: 'All peoples on earth will be blessed through you' (Genesis 12:3).

# God's reign brings justice

God's reign makes real the prophets' promise of a world of justice and peace. 'The last will be first, and the first will be last' (Matthew 20:16) is a saying of Jesus which sums up his vision of a world where all that is upside down will be put right. This is why his 'good news for the poor' had such electrifying effect. It would mean bad news for the rich and comfortable:

Happy are you poor,
the Kingdom of God is yours!
Happy are you who are hungry now;
you will be filled! . . .
But how terrible for you who are rich now;
you have had your easy life!
How terrible for you who are full now;
you will go hungry!

(Luke 6:20–25, GNB)

Justice would mean that the huge inequalities of human society would be put right. No wonder the poor hung on Jesus' words, and the self-satisfied felt threatened by him.

'The poor' for whom Jesus brings good news are the people who are without power, people who count for little in the world's eyes. In Jesus' time they would include widows, orphans, refugees, the disabled, and people who were despised because they did dirty jobs or benefited from the Roman occupation of Palestine. Jesus came to show that God has a new deal for them.

Every society has people whom it would prefer not to be there. It may be the misfits who sleep rough under the railway arches, or the uncared-for and insecure young people who display their anger in violence around the neighbourhood. In some cities of the Two-Thirds World it is the street children, whose numbers the authorities control by having them shot like rabbits.

But Jesus wasn't announcing a peasants' revolt or a class war. He wasn't calling people to rebel against the established power. He was telling them what *God* was doing. And even though he was undoubtedly for the poor, he wasn't against the rich. There is good news for them too, though they may find it hard to hear. God's love has no favourites. He makes the sun shine and the rain fall on good and bad alike, and 'he is kind to the ungrateful and wicked' (Matthew 5:45; Luke 6:35). Jesus was as ready to eat with a religious leader as with a tax-collector, as ready to heal the daughter of a synagogue official as a leprosy sufferer.

Now of course Jesus didn't magically get the poor out of poverty or plant the outcast at the centre of respectable society. But he welcomed them into a new community. People who had been battered by circumstances were accepted and valued in a new way. Those who had been gripped by evil habits were set free by the power of his love. Nobodies became somebodies. They discovered in Jesus a whole new world of possibilities. They found in each other a circle of acceptance which enabled them to believe that life was worth living again. They gave themselves to Jesus' mission of sharing the good news of God's reign. The revolution was under way.

## God's reign demands our response

Jesus' message about God's reign was mostly about the new world which God was creating. But it was also about the response which God's reign demands. God's reign is some-thing which has to be entered. It is a gift which has to be received. 'I tell you the truth, anyone who will not receive the kingdom of God [that is, his reign] like a little child will never enter it' (Mark 10:15).

Jesus liked to compare a would-be follower to a child. Children are dependent. They know when they need help. They are wide-eyed with wonder at the possibilities of life. They receive with open arms a gift which is offered. Unless you are willing to leave behind your idea that you can make it on your own and put yourself into the hands of God, Jesus says, you can't be my disciple.

God became real and central in my life when I heard someone talking about this story which Jesus told. God's reign, said Jesus, 'is like a merchant looking for fine pearls. When he found one of great value, he went away and sold everything he had and bought it' (Matthew 13:45–46).

I felt like the merchant discovering the blessings of God's reign after a long search. And I saw that this treasure of infinite value demanded everything I could give. Total offer, total demand. I opened my life to a relationship with God. I committed myself, as best I knew how, to living in obedience to the demands of his reign. And I was overwhelmed by an awareness of his love.

When diamonds were first discovered in Hopetown, South Africa, experts refused to believe the evidence. A mineralogist sent out from London suggested that if a diamond were found in that region it must have been carried there in the gizzard of an ostrich. He even dismissed a magnificent white diamond known today as 'the Star of Africa' and worth millions.

There were contemporaries of Jesus who had the evidence of his teaching, his miracles and the change he brought to people's lives. And they said in effect, 'This isn't God at work. It's Satan deceiving people' (see Mark 3:22). There are people today confronted by similar evidence. But they will share in its blessings only if, in simple trust, they respond to Jesus' invitation to enter God's reign and to take upon themselves its demands.

## God's reign is still coming

There's one other part of Jesus' message: God's reign hasn't yet fully come. The Jesus who captivated his hearers in Nazareth with news of its dawning also taught his followers to pray, 'May your reign come.' The coming of God's reign isn't a once-for-all event. What God's people longed for, through all those years of waiting, came in part through what Jesus did in Galilee and in Jerusalem. But its complete coming remains an object of hope.

Through Jesus' life, death and resurrection, God's reign was brought near to us. Its effects were seen in the miraculous events of his ministry and the changed lives of his followers. God's mission statement was being put into effect in a decisive way which would direct the shape of all subsequent human history.

The American journalist Lincoln Steffens visited Russia in the early days after the Marxist revolution of 1917. He came back with the triumphant report: 'I have seen the future and it works.' After the collapse of communist rule in the Soviet Union and eastern Europe in 1989, we know differently. But the slogan is one which Christians can use as we look at the impact of Jesus in his own time and on the peoples of the world.

God is moving forward in his plan to create a new world of justice and peace, of love and celebration, under his rule. Every time we see a Christian community truly living by the values of his reign we can say, 'I have seen the future and it works.'

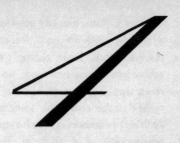

# THE COMING OF CHRIST

'In the beginning was the creation. Now scientists try again.'
My eyes were drawn to the newspaper headline, and the
photo of the CERN particle generator in Switzerland. It
announced triumphantly that, in an underground warren of
tunnels and cables, physicists have reproduced the Big Bang
with which the universe began 15 billion years ago. Well,
they haven't exactly reproduced it. But they've managed to
make a handful of particles survive for a few billionths of a
second.

Humanity's destiny is to think God's thoughts after him.
Sometimes we kid ourselves that we're doing rather well at
replacing him. But somehow we don't quite manage the same
spectacular effects. We've also come close in recent decades to
bringing the world as we know it to an end. Fortunately, our
efforts at this enterprise too have had limited consequences,
and we survive to explore alternative futures.

The truth is that neither the beginning nor the end is
subject to merely human control. Over all our human stories
is God's great story, his 'mission', as we described it in

chapter 3. And, like any good story, his story has a beginning, a middle and an end. Its centre is the life, death and resurrection of Jesus, through whom God came near to men and women in a new way, and sent the shockwaves of his reign rippling through history.

And from there the story goes on. The series of Jesus' visible appearances on earth came to an end six weeks after his resurrection. But then at Pentecost God's Spirit came, enabling Jesus' followers to continue the work he had begun. Through two thousand years they have shared the good news of God's care for all the world. Despite frequent compromises and sheer failure to live up to the Christian vision, at their best they have relied on God's strength and struggled for God's goals. They have lived and died by God's 'mission statement', his plan 'to bring all creation together, everything in heaven and on earth, with Christ as head' (Ephesians 1:10, GNB).

## Jesus and the future

God intends to see that plan through to its completion. Jesus crammed a lot of his vision of the future into one brief picture:

> I say to you that many will come from the east and the west, and will take their places at the feast with Abraham, Isaac and Jacob in the kingdom of heaven.       (Matthew 8:11)

Here he looked forward to the time when God's reign would finally arrive in its completeness. He describes this reign as a feast, a party. That's always a good start! It's not about being solemnly religious, but about celebration. It's the overflowing excitement of people caught up in God's plan for the world. Like students celebrating their graduation, or football fans whose team has at last won the Cup, they know that the hard work has been done and the goal achieved.

Jesus also makes clear that God's reign stretches back to include those in whom the vision was first born, like Abraham and his sons, and those who kept the light aflame when darkness seemed all around. But now – and this came as a shock to those of his own people who thought that non-Jews were always outside the range of God's interest – his reign will embrace people of all races. God's rainbow people will unite in celebration. All will live in harmony under God's just and gentle rule. The dream of the Hebrew prophets will at last come true.

What Jesus spoke of in pictures and brief sayings was developed by New Testament writers who wrote from the other side of his resurrection. They spoke of his 'coming'. They used the old picture of 'the day of the Lord', which for Old Testament prophets meant a decisive and possibly final act of God in history, and which now pointed to the coming of Christ as Lord to bring God's plan for the world to its goal. The unknown writer of the letter to Hebrew Christians put it like this:

> Christ was sacrificed once to take away the sins of many people; and he will appear a second time, not to bear sin, but to bring salvation to those who are waiting for him.
>
> (Hebrews 9:28)

Most of the questions which might be asked about the final coming of Jesus fall into the categories of 'How?' 'When?' and 'Why?' A lot of energy is often spent on arguing about how and when Jesus will come. But the most important question is 'Why?'

# Why will Jesus come?

What is the purpose of his coming? What truths about God and his plans for the world is this message meant to safeguard? Let's look at three main reasons.

## *Jesus will complete his work*

First, Jesus will come to complete what he began in Bethlehem and Galilee and Jerusalem. Without his final coming God's story has a beginning and a middle, but no end. Or, as theologian Emil Brunner put it:

> Faith in Jesus without the expectation of his final coming is a cheque that is never cashed, a promise that is not made in earnest. A faith in Christ without the expectation of his coming is like a flight of stairs which leads nowhere, but ends in the void.

Jesus began his work in Galilee announcing: 'The Kingdom of God is near! Turn away from your sins and believe the Good News!' (Mark 1:15, GNB). He pointed to the presence of God's reign in the effects of his preaching and healing. Yet he urged his followers to pray for God's reign still to come in its completeness – 'Your kingdom come' (Luke 11:2). The whole New Testament is permeated with this sense of 'already . . . but not yet'. Christ has already come to bring God's reign close to us, and he will come again to bring God's reign in all its fullness.

Many churches celebrate the prospect of Christ's future coming at the same time as we begin to prepare for Christmas – the season of Advent. In practice this often means that the future hope gets lost beneath the tinsel and the Christmas puddings. But it is intended to make the crucial point that the two comings of Jesus belong together. The final coming of Christ is not an optional extra or a bizarre idea promoted by fanatics, but a vital part of normal Christian understanding about the significance of Jesus.

This leads directly to a further point. When we say, 'He will come again', we are affirming that the one to come is the Jesus whom we know from the Bible and from history and from his impact on our own experience. The 'second coming' is not an event but a person – a person whose arms, stretched out on the cross, express his constant commitment to the well-being of all humanity.

## *Jesus will bring judgment and abolish evil*

Secondly, Jesus' coming will mean judgment on all people. When the Lord comes 'he will bring to light what is hidden in darkness and will expose the motives of people's hearts' (1 Corinthians 4:5). We like to think that we are independent, free, able to make choices in life without worrying about the consequences. Especially for comfortable westerners, who don't normally find themselves on the receiving end of injustice, the idea of a God of justice has become alien to our patterns of thought. But if you're the victim of injustice, if the whole system is stacked against you, you long for justice and you long to know that the unjust will not get away with their injustice for ever.

So the message of God's judgment warns us that one day all our over-inflated ideas about ourselves will burst like soap-bubbles, and we shall be seen as we truly are. And it tells us that in the end, God's justice will prevail. The Hitlers and the Saddam Husseins of this world will answer for their crimes, and each nameless victim of oppression will meet the God who sets the broken victims free.

When Jesus comes all evil will be brought to an end.

Everything which spoils God's world and makes us less than God meant us to be will be finished for ever. Paul writes that Christ 'must reign until he has put all his enemies under his feet' (1 Corinthians 15:25). At his first coming, Jesus engaged in battle with those enemies – evil, fear, suffering and death. At his final coming, his victory will be complete. Never again will the clock be turned back to a world ravaged by evil.

Jesus will then welcome his people into the permanent presence of God. 'He will send his angels and gather his elect [his chosen ones] from the four winds, from the ends of the earth to the ends of the heavens' (Mark 13:27). He will draw together both the dead and the living into his new world of justice and love. The God whose goal is to bring all creation together with Christ as Head will stop at nothing short of that.

## Jesus will renew creation

Thirdly, Jesus' coming will bring the renewal of creation. Contrary to popular opinion, the Bible does not speak of 'the end of the world' so much as of 'a new heaven and a new earth'. It doesn't speak of people simply abandoning the earth and 'going to heaven', but of God transforming the whole created environment. Paul, for example, writes that the universe itself is waiting to be 'liberated from its bondage to decay and brought into the glorious freedom of the children of God' (Romans 8:21). The liberation of God's people into life with God is bound up with the transformation of the whole created order.

In similar vein John the prophet 'saw a new heaven and a new earth' and 'heard a loud voice from the throne saying, "Now the dwelling of God is with human beings, and he will live with them. They will be his people, and God himself will be with them"' (Revelation 21:1, 3). Then the story will be complete. God's intention to be friends with his human creatures, announced in the Garden of Eden in Genesis 2 – 3, will be realized in a permanent relationship.

## How will Jesus come?

The question 'How will Jesus come?' is more easily asked than answered. Some passages in the New Testament suggest a quite straightforward answer. Imagine you are standing on the Mount of Olives near Jerusalem with those who have worked with Jesus during his ministry. With them you are gazing into the sky, wondering what has happened to the risen Jesus who, a few moments ago, was speaking with you in his final appearance after his resurrection. Suddenly you are conscious of two angelic figures standing beside you.

'Why do you stand here looking into the sky?' they ask. 'This same Jesus, who has been taken from you into heaven, will come back in the same way you have seen him go into heaven' (Acts 1:11).

It sounds simple. If Jesus left the earth from the Mount of Olives, he will return one day to the same place. His return will be like a film of his ascension played backwards. And that's exactly how many people understand it. If this were the only way in which New Testament writers described the coming of Christ, such an approach might be justified. But in fact a wide range of description is found, some of it much more symbolic and allusive.

Some kinds of events can't be described with ordinary straightforward words. At really big moments in our lives – what it feels like to fall in love, perhaps, or the experience of becoming a parent for the first time – we struggle to find words. Tidy statements are totally inadequate. We turn to the language of poetry, which speaks less precisely yet gets closer to the heart of the matter. W. H. Auden's expression of love, made famous in the film *Four Weddings and a Funeral*, tells you nothing about the person described and everything about his impact on the lover:

> He was my North, my South, my East and West,
> My working week and my Sunday rest,
> My moon, my midnight, my talk, my song . . .

Biblical writers too use the language of poetry and symbol when describing really big events. 'All the trees of the field will clap their hands' (Isaiah 55:12) hardly describes a new mutation in the natural world, which will draw the crowds to the Botanical Gardens. It's poetic language conveying the drama of a new act of God.

And when depicting future events of a kind never experienced before, it's no surprise that they call on a range of imagery which refuses to be pinned down. Like the resurrection of Jesus, his final coming is not merely an event in history. It touches history, but is at the same time beyond history. If we try to remove the element of mystery from it, we are ceasing to live by faith and are trying to live by sight.

But this doesn't mean we can say nothing about how Christ will come. New Testament writers bring out three aspects of it.

## Jesus will come suddenly

First, Jesus' coming will be sudden. Jesus pictured a man devastated by a burglary:

> If the owner of the house had known at what time of night the thief was coming, he would have kept watch and would not have let his house be broken into. So you also must be

ready, because the Son of Man will come at an hour when you do not expect him.

> (Matthew 24:43–44; 'the Son of Man'
> is a phrase used by Jesus to refer to himself)

Peter Smith played cricket for Essex. In a match against Yorkshire in 1935 he fielded throughout the two Yorkshire innings without the ball ever coming near him. Then Yorkshire's last batsman skied a catch. And he was alert to take the catch and win the game.

Christ's coming will be sudden and unexpected. At any time he may confront us with his demanding presence. We can never settle down to live as though it could safely be confined to the remote future. His coming affects us now because its timing cannot be predicted.

## Jesus will come triumphantly

Secondly, in contrast with his first coming, Christ's final coming will be public and triumphant. He once crept into the world almost unnoticed. His identity remained a matter of debate. He was rejected and crucified by people in power. And even then he was hardly big enough news to hit the headlines. The Roman historian Tacitus, describing events in Palestine at that time, wrote: 'Under Tiberius all was quiet.'

Not next time! The Son of Man will come 'in clouds with great power and glory' (Mark 13:26). This kind of imagery shows that he will come in triumph, with the full authority of God behind him. Through his suffering he has conquered the power of evil. At his coming he will show that his victory is complete, as 'every tongue' confesses that 'Jesus Christ is Lord, to the glory of God the Father' (Philippians 2:11).

Thirdly, his coming will be glorious and universal in its impact. It will be no mere local manifestation, for 'every eye will see him' (Revelation 1:7). Jesus himself said: 'As lightning that comes from the east is visible even in the west, so will be the coming of the Son of Man' (Matthew 24:27). No-one will miss it. It will be nothing less than 'the glorious appearing of our great God and Saviour, Jesus Christ' (Titus 2:13). We may think that World Cup football or the Olympic Games, watched by half the world on TV, are big events. But the razzmatazz of such events is nothing compared with the impact of the coming of Christ.

## When will Jesus come?

Does the fact that history has gone on so long since the time of Christ cast doubt on the first Christians' expectation of his return? That question was already raised in New Testament times. The second letter of Peter refers to cynics who say, 'Where is this "coming" he promised? Ever since our ancestors died, everything goes on as it has since the beginning of creation' (2 Peter 3:4).

Weren't the first Christians just whistling in the dark, pinning their hopes on good times in the future to get them through bad times in the present? Doesn't the fact that people have been hoping for Christ's coming without success for 2,000 years suggest that their belief was mistaken all along? And isn't it enough anyway to believe that individuals live after their death, without all this expectation of Christ coming to earth again in the future? Let's begin with that last question.

The hope of Christ's final coming safeguards a number of

important truths. It reminds us, first, that God is passionately committed to the world he has made. His liberation of humanity doesn't consist simply in his rescuing us out of the world. Christ came to defeat the evil in the world, and his coming will demonstrate in the world that his mission is successfully completed.

Secondly, God's plans don't just involve the human race, but affect the rest of creation too.

And thirdly, God is moving human history towards a goal. The Christian message isn't about God lifting a select group of people out of history into heaven, but about God working with the ups and downs of history towards his grand finale. Imagine a football game where no-one blows the final whistle, or a race in which there is no finishing-tape and the athletes gradually drop out exhausted. Without the focus on Christ's final coming, the history of the world would be like a meaningless game, an uncompleted sentence, a puzzle with no solution.

## *The timing of Jesus' coming*

It is sometimes said that the first followers of Jesus were expecting him to come again within a short time after his death, and that they must have felt disillusioned when he didn't. But there is no evidence of such disappointment in the New Testament documents. That taunt in 2 Peter comes from outside the Christian community. And the writer's response is that such critics simply don't understand God's timescale, or appreciate that he is generously allowing time for the cynics to learn the error of their ways.

It is true that New Testament writers sometimes expressed themselves as though they believed that Christ might come very soon. Paul, for example, wrote to his friends in Thessalonica:

> We who are still alive, who are left till the coming of the
> Lord, will certainly not precede those who have fallen asleep.
>
> (1 Thessalonians 4:15)

And a saying of Jesus himself has sometimes been taken to
mean that he expected the final coming of God's reign within
a generation:

> Some who are standing here will not taste death before they see
> the kingdom [the reign] of God come with power. (Mark 9:1)

But Paul's statement merely proves that he reckoned with
the *possibility* of Christ coming in the near future. He could
hardly have written, 'We who will die before the coming of
the Lord', since that would commit him to the view that
Christ would not return till some time later. And Jesus'
saying probably doesn't refer to his final coming at all. It
asserts that before long, some at least of those around him
would recognize the powerful reign of God at work in the
world – for example, through his resurrection and the coming
of God's Spirit at Pentecost.

New Testament writers, like every biblical prophet, spoke
of God's activity in the future with a vividness which made it
sound very near. That was the job of a prophet – to speak of
God's future in a way which brings home its impact on the
present. They proclaimed that the climax of history would
come suddenly. It *might* be soon. But what mattered was not
its timing but the certainty that its coming was guaranteed by
a God who keeps his promises. In their expectation they were
not like the NASA scientist precisely counting down the
seconds to lift-off. They were more like the child who 'can't
wait' for Christmas to come but is too young to know how to
count the days.

But was their hope just wishful thinking, a nice idea with no solid base to support it? It might be thought so, except for one thing. On a Sunday morning around AD 30, Jesus was raised from death by the power of God. The tomb was empty, and he appeared over a period of time to groups of his followers. He restored their shattered dreams and launched a new power into the world. Unless Jesus was raised from the grave, the survival and dynamic growth of the movement which he started form a mystery without a solution. There is no other adequate explanation.

The resurrection of Jesus from the grave is the foundation of all our hope for the future. In this resurrection God has set his seal of approval on the Jesus who came to announce God's reign. He has guaranteed his promise to bring his reign in its totality through the final coming of Jesus. In this one resurrection within history God has demonstrated his commitment to offer resurrection to all at the end of history.

But are there *no* clues as to when it might happen? We'll look at this more closely in the next chapter.

# THE TIME, THE PLACE

---

We've looked at the why and how of Christ's coming, and have started to think about the when. Some people think Jesus' return is imminent. Why do they get so excited about the year 2000?

Let televangelist Jack Van Impe speak for them. According to his video message, *AD 2000 . . . The End?*, it all starts from 2 Peter 3:8 – 'With the Lord a day is like a thousand years, and a thousand years are like a day.' Now, since the world was made in seven days, it's fitting that it should last for 7,000 years. He reckons that Adam was created 4,000 years before Christ. So after 2,000 years of Christian history we're now ready for the seventh 'day' – Jesus' coming followed by his 1,000-year reign on earth, the 'millennium'.

And there's another way of reaching the same conclusion, says Van Impe. The year 1948 saw the return of Israel to its homeland. And, according to Scripture, the End will come within one generation of that significant event.

'That comes out, folks, to the year 2000!' declares Van Impe, like a magician pulling a rabbit out of a hat. He got there by a complicated calculation which concluded that in the Bible a generation is 51.4 years. So, as near as makes no difference, he's got to the year 2000.

'I'm not a date-setter,' he assures us. 'We don't know the day nor the hour. But we can know the time when Christ is right at the door.'

You don't have to be a super-cynic to feel that there are a few questionable assumptions in these calculations. But add to them the general sense of foreboding about world events as the new millennium approaches. Throw in also the hype of governments and commercial interests eager to cash in on this never-to-be-repeated moment, and you have a rich cocktail of anticipation.

## Biblical arithmetic

Those who focus on the timing of Christ's coming have two main methods of calculation. The first approach uses biblical numbers. In 1842 William Miller, a self-educated New England farmer, wrote: 'I am fully convinced that somewhere between March 21st, 1843, and March 21st, 1844, according to the Jewish mode of computation of time, Christ will come.' Already a preacher with a modest following, he found now that his prediction raised audiences to thousands and expectations to fever pitch. But why 1843?

He got there by combining two texts in the book of Daniel. In the Authorized Version, Daniel 9:24 says: 'Seventy weeks are determined upon thy people . . . to make an end of sins.' Miller interpreted seventy weeks, or 490 days, as meaning 490 years. And he took the 'end of sins' to refer to Christ's crucifixion, which he dated in AD 33. Count back 490 years from AD 33 and you get to 457 BC. Now read Daniel 8:14: '. . . unto two thousand and three hundred days; then shall the sanctuary be cleansed' (AV). Count the 2,300 days (= years) forward from 457 BC and you arrive at AD 1843. In that year, said Miller, the earth would be 'cleansed' as Christ's rule on earth began. A series of other calculations led him to the twelve months beginning on 21 March of that year.

When 21 March 1844 came and went, he adjusted the deadline to 22 October. That also proved a non-event, and there followed what became known as the Great Disappointment. Amazingly, Miller's following continued to increase and was the spiritual root of movements such as the Seventh Day Adventists and the Jehovah's Witnesses.

This last group predicted the end of the present world for 1874, 1878, 1881, 1910, 1914, 1918, 1925, 1975 and 1984, until finally in 1996 they announced that they had given up precise calculations. In view of their track record, it was probably a wise decision.

These and many other failed attempts should be enough to discredit the method. The truth is that the numbers in Daniel are contradictory and confusing if taken literally. They have symbolic meaning rather than stopwatch precision. The seventy weeks in Daniel 9:24, for example, don't refer literally to 490 years. They mean that God's purposes for his people will surely be fulfilled, since seven signifies completeness.

Jesus said, 'No-one knows about that day or hour, not even the angels in heaven, nor the Son, but only the Father' (Mark 13:32). Moreover, he actually condemned date-fixing by numbers. Some Pharisees asked him when the kingdom of God would come. He answered, 'The kingdom of God does not come with careful observation' (Luke 17:20). He was rejecting the view, which was popular among some Pharisees at the time, that the coming of the Messiah could be precisely dated with the help of numbers from the book of Daniel.

A more familiar method of working out the date relies on the 'signs of the times' described by Jesus in Mark 13 (also in Matthew 24 and Luke 21). One day, during the final week of his earthly life, Jesus was leaving the Jerusalem temple. 'Look!' said his friends. 'Aren't they magnificent buildings!'

'You see these great buildings?' Jesus replied. 'Not one stone here will be left on another. Every one will be thrown down.'

Soon afterwards they pressed their questions on him. 'When will this happen? What will be the sign that it's all about to come true?'

Jesus replied not with 'a sign' but with a bewildering range of 'signs'. He spoke of false messiahs, war, earthquakes, famine, the persecution of his followers as they announce the good news about him, and attacks on Jerusalem and its temple. And then there would be disturbances among sun, moon and stars, and the glorious appearing of the Son of Man.

It's not difficult for a preacher to hold up a Bible in one hand and a newspaper in the other and say, 'Look, all these things are happening in our time. So get ready! Christ is coming any day now.'

But Jesus can hardly have meant these 'signs' to be indicators that the End would be just round the next corner. Such things have gone on right through history. And there is no evidence that disasters are more frequent now than in earlier periods. Jesus was telling his disciples to expect them right from Day 1.

## *'These things', 'those days', and 'that day'*

There is in fact a change of focus from Mark 13:23 to the next verse. Hold tight while we go into a few details here! Verses

6–23 survey those conflicts and upheavals which soon became familiar to Jesus' early followers. They are these things which the disciples asked about (verse 4). The main focus is on events leading up to the destruction of Jerusalem by the Romans, which took place in AD 70. While similar things have gone on throughout history, Jesus' main point here was to stress the urgency of being prepared for that catastrophe which was to confront Jerusalem and the Jewish people.

Then verse 24 begins, 'But in those days, following that distress . . .' emphasizing that a later time is now being highlighted. Now (verses 24–27) Jesus speaks of his final coming in glory. He does not say that the earthquakes, false messiahs and other disasters will show that his coming is about to happen. He clearly distinguishes between 'these things' (events of the first century) and 'those days' (the time of his coming again).

Then comes a short parable.

> Learn this lesson from the fig-tree: As soon as its twigs get tender and its leaves come out, you know that summer is near. Even so, when you see these things happening, you know that it is near, right at the door. I tell you the truth, this generation will certainly not pass away until all these things have happened. (Mark 13:28–30)

Once again, 'these things' and 'all these things' refer to the first-century events rather than to Jesus' final coming.

Finally in verse 32 Jesus says, 'No-one knows about that day' – the day of his coming. Throughout the passage, the distinction is kept between 'these things' and 'those days' or 'that day'. The timing of 'that day' remains unpredictable. You can't work it out from the 'signs' which Jesus described earlier.

In fact, the whole point of Jesus' teaching here wasn't to encourage calculation, but to strengthen faith and to warn of dangers that his followers could expect. When such things happen, we shouldn't imagine that God has lost control or that his plan has gone off course.

The so-called 'signs' are not like the road signs which announce 'End of motorway 1 mile'. They are like the hazard warning signs which alert us to dangers along the way. Jesus isn't inviting prediction but encouraging faithfulness. Repeatedly in Mark 13 he warns: 'Watch out', 'Do not be alarmed', 'Be on your guard', 'Do not worry', 'If anyone says to you, "Look, here is the Christ!" do not believe it', 'Be alert', 'Keep watch.' And he promises: 'Whoever stands firm to the end will be saved' (Matthew 24:13). That's the message which Christians today should take from these chapters.

## Madmen and messiahs

We've seen all too vividly in recent years what happens when the wrong use of Scripture is combined with powerful personalities. In 1987 David Koresh took charge of the Branch Davidians in Waco, Texas. They made money buying and selling guns, and stockpiled for themselves a huge supply of firearms and ammunition.

Koresh claimed to receive direct instructions from God, and taught that he himself was the 'lamb' of Revelation 5 – the only one able to open the 'seven seals' and unleash the events which would lead to the world's final judgment and the flight of the group to heaven. But the law-enforcement authorities had other ideas.

In April 1993, after a seven-week siege, the FBI went in. No-one knows how the fire started. Relatives of group members in several parts of the world watched on TV as buildings went up in flames. Twenty-one children and fifty-three adults, including David Koresh, died.

Of the nine who escaped that day, most were still obsessed three years later with Koresh's interpretation of the seven seals. They believed him to be the Son of God who would soon return to raise the dead. The resurrection was scheduled for 13 December 1996 . . .

Less loaded with tragedy is the story of Lee Jang Rim, who persuaded 20,000 Koreans to expect to be 'raptured' to heaven at midnight on 29 October 1992. To prepare for Jesus' arrival to meet them, they gave up jobs, sold houses, and handed over assets to nice Mr Lee. Some women even had abortions so that they wouldn't be too heavy to be lifted up to heaven!

But the police have a part in this story too. Lee was sentenced to two years' imprisonment for defrauding believers of $4 million and illegally possessing $26,711 in United States currency. Most embarrassing for Lee was that some of the money was in the form of bonds not due to mature until 1995. That persuaded the court that Lee's motives weren't entirely spiritual.

If there is a lesson to be learnt from these stories, it is that a little bit of doubt, a willingness to ask questions, is a vital part of real faith. Few things are more dangerous than the combination of a powerful leader and unquestioning, adoring disciples. 'A madman can look a lot like a messiah,' declared one newspaper headline over the Waco story.

On the morning after the day scheduled for Lee Jang Rim's promised 'rapture', one of his aides announced to the faithful gathered in Seoul churches, 'Nothing has happened. Sorry. Let's go home.' They were lucky to get an apology. The Branch Davidians had no such luxury.

# The Great Tribulation

A popular view of the future leans heavily on the books of Daniel and Revelation. It is the view of most American televangelists and of most paperbacks on the Christian hope to be found in evangelical bookshops. It goes like this.

Sometime in the near future all true Christians will be suddenly caught up into heaven to be with Christ. This is the 'secret rapture', which this school of thought finds in 1 Thessalonians 4:13–18, which speaks of Christians being 'caught up' to meet with Christ in the air. This will be followed by a seven-year period of conflict and catastrophe on the earth, the 'Great Tribulation' of Matthew 24:21, from which Christians are exempt.

The books of Revelation (chapters 6 – 19) and Daniel (chapter 7 and 9:24–27) describe what will happen during this period. The Antichrist, a powerful dictator, will emerge as the head of a ten-nation European confederation, with its capital in Rome. The basis of this is the fact that in Revelation 13:1, the Beast (the Antichrist) echoes the fourth kingdom of Daniel 7, which is interpreted as the Roman Empire.

The European Union was founded through the Treaty of Rome in 1957 and is therefore the revived Roman empire foreseen by the biblical writers. Since the Beast has ten horns, this new Roman Empire must consist of ten nations. So somehow the membership of the EU has to be got back down to ten before the prophecy can come true.

The Antichrist will persecute any who try to resist him (Revelation 13:5–7). Armies from the Arab world, Russia and Africa will in turn converge on the Middle East, until Russia is utterly defeated by the European forces (Daniel 11:40–45). Then, in a final battle at Armageddon (Megiddo, in northern Israel), huge forces from China (the 200 million of Revelation

9:16) and the European confederation will meet head-on (Revelation 16:16). But at the climax of this terrible battle Christ will return to judge the godless nations (Revelation 19:19–21).

Christ will then begin a 1,000-year reign over those who are left on earth. At the end of this period Satan will be allowed a brief repeat of his destructive role before being destroyed for ever (Revelation 20:1–10). After the last judgment (Revelation 20:11–15), there will be the new heaven and new earth in which God's people will live for ever in his presence (Revelation 21 – 22).

There are multiple variations in this scheme, endlessly adjusted to fit with events in the Six-Day War of 1967, the Yom Kippur War of 1973, the collapse of the Soviet Union in 1989, the Gulf War of 1990, and however many members the European Union happens to have at any particular time.

And mixed in with it are all those details pointed out to confirm that 'the Bible is as up-to-date as tomorrow's newspaper – if you follow my interpretation'. The locusts of Revelation 9:3–11, 'whatever they represent, will be much larger than ordinary locusts and they will not look like the locust of today', wrote Salem Kirban in 1968. No, actually they are Cobra helicopters spraying nerve gas from their tails (Hal Lindsey, 1973). No, they're killer bees from South America (Kirban again, 1977).

And then there's the Beast in chapter 13, who decrees that no-one may take part in the economic system unless they have his number, 666, marked on their hand or forehead. So there are people who refuse to have those numbers on their cheque book or bank card. Some are paranoid about barcodes. Others warn that the technology now exists to impose personal identification numbers by means of invisible laser tattoos, or by silicon chips implanted beneath the skin. And some mathematical genius has discovered that if you attach numerical values to the letters of the alphabet, so that A=6, B=12, C=18, and so on, the word COMPUTER adds up to 666. Now we know the source of all our troubles!

## Weighing the evidence

To be serious, this whole scheme rests on a questionable understanding of a small number of biblical passages, mostly in books whose use of picture language makes precise interpretation difficult anyway. The scheme is attractive because it appears to take the details of Scripture seriously and to offer a certainty about the future which people long for. Other people may seek such certainty in horoscopes. Many Christians seek it through detailed schemes of prophetic interpretation confidently proclaimed by authoritative teachers.

The scheme is open to question at a number of points. First, the 'secret rapture'. Those who hold this view are committed to belief in *two* future comings of Jesus – one to whisk believers from the earth to heaven before the Great Tribulation, the other after the Tribulation to begin his reign on earth. But elsewhere, New Testament writers frequently link the welcoming of believers into Christ's presence, the final judgment and the completion of all God's plans to the one final coming of Jesus. There is no hint of two comings, and no sane reason for finding it in 1 Thessalonians 4.

Secondly, there's the notion that believers will be safely off the scene before the worst sufferings in history occur. There is no support for it in the Bible, which constantly insists that Christians are preserved not *from* suffering but *through* it. 'We must go through many hardships [AV "much tribulation"] to enter the kingdom of God' (Acts 14:22). It's no argument to say that the church isn't mentioned in Revelation 4 – 19, and therefore the church has been removed from earth beforehand. The word 'church' isn't used there, but the church certainly features there, symbolized by the two witnesses in chapter 11 and the woman and her offspring in chapter 12.

Thirdly, the confident identification of references to ancient countries and places with their modern counterparts gives the impression of a precision which Scripture simply doesn't provide. Russia gets in on the act mainly because of descriptions in Ezekiel 38 and Daniel 11 of Israel's enemies sweeping down from the north. But the geography of the region dictated that Israel's traditional enemies, such as Assyria and Babylon, always attacked from the north. So the reference to an attack from the north doesn't point to a specific modern nation located due north of Israel.

Fourthly, we can raise questions about the idea of a revived Roman Empire. This involves more problems than just the unlikelihood of the European Union having exactly ten members. Clearly, for the author of Revelation, the Beast *did* symbolize Rome. But if we then 'transfer' Rome to a period 2,000 years later, we make the book irrelevant to its first readers. The anxious and threatened Christians for whom John wrote are being cheated out of a word from God.

And Armageddon isn't as straightforward as it seems. Yes, the plain of Megiddo has been a notable battlefield from the fifteenth century BC to the First World War, so it would be no surprise to see another battle in that setting. But the word 'Armageddon' appears to mean 'Mountain of Megiddo', and the place is certainly not a mountain.

John's very choice of word suggests that he isn't trying to describe an actual military battle with forces from Europe and the East. Armageddon is a symbol for the climactic conflict between Christ and all who oppose his will. Revelation constantly uses the imagery of battle to describe the victory of

Christ and his people over their enemies. 'To him who overcomes' or 'whoever conquers' is a refrain in each of the letters to the seven churches. But their fighting and their victory, like that of Christ himself, are conducted with weapons of love and suffering rather than with force of arms.

Finally, what may we say about the millennium of Revelation 20, a 'Satan-free' period during which Christian martyrs reign with Christ for 1,000 years? If we had no other New Testament books but this one, it might be natural to see this as a future period following the triumphant return of Christ portrayed in Revelation 19:11–21. The strength of this view (known as 'premillennialism') is its insistence that God, who has been committed throughout history to working out his rescue plan on this earth, should demonstrate on earth his ultimate victory.

But in Jesus' and Paul's teaching about God's reign, there seems to be no 'gap' into which such a 1,000-year period could be fitted. In their perspective, there are 'this age' and 'the age to come', with the final coming of Christ marking the boundary between the two. So it's better to interpret the millennium as a symbolic description of Christ reigning *now*, between his first and final comings ('amillennialism'). As Paul writes, the risen Christ 'must reign until he has put all his enemies under his feet' (1 Corinthians 15:25).

But dogmatism isn't a valid option in this matter. However precisely we interpret it, John's real point is that those who have lost most in this world – the Christian martyrs – have in truth lost nothing. They have gained everything because they live in Christ's presence and share in his reign. Evil can touch them no longer and Christ's triumph is complete.

## Fatalism in disguise?

I will say more about what I believe the book of Revelation *does* have to say in chapter 7. For now I simply comment that the view which I have criticized fails to do justice to the situation of its first readers, or to the picture language which it uses. It fails to interpret Revelation in relation to the clearer teaching of Jesus and the other New Testament writers. It points attention away from Christ and all that he has already done to bring God's reign to earth. It doesn't stir Christians to compassionate care for the world, but paralyses them. What it offers isn't hope but a kind of fatalism disguised as hope.

# GOOD NEWS FOR THE JEWS

The steady trickle of Jews to settle in Palestine, which began in the nineteenth century and rose to a flood in the 1940s, is one of the most remarkable phenomena of modern history. The establishment and preservation of the State of Israel since 1948 is seen by many as nothing short of miraculous. For many Christians, 1948 marks a significant moment in 'God's prophetic count-down' towards the return of Christ. So we need to ask whether this is, as many claim, the greatest sign of all that the coming of Christ can't be delayed much longer. The reasons for their mounting excitement go something like this.

God promised Abraham, 'The whole land of Canaan . . . I will give as an everlasting possession to you and your descendants' (Genesis 17:8). This promise was to be fulfilled through the Israelites descended from Abraham's son Isaac, rather than through his son Ishmael, from whom sprang the Arab race (Genesis 17:19–21).

In line with this, there are promises in the Hebrew prophets that Jews dispersed from their land will one day be brought back to it to experience afresh the blessings of God.

Those promises have been dramatically fulfilled, particularly since 1948.

Two particular statements of Jesus are often added. The first is the parable about the fig tree (Mark 13:28–30), already mentioned in chapter 5. Now the fig tree in the Bible is sometimes a picture of Israel. So Jesus is taken to mean that when Israel 'grows leaves again' (blossoms again in the Holy Land) the 'summer' of Christ's return is just round the corner. The generation living at that time will survive to see his coming. So it can hardly be delayed beyond the year 2000.

The second statement is in Luke 21:24, where Jesus speaks of the destruction of Jerusalem by the Romans – which was to take place in AD 70 – and adds: 'Jerusalem will be trampled on by the Gentiles until the times of the Gentiles are fulfilled.' He then goes on to describe his final coming. So now that Gentile control of the land – and of Jerusalem itself since the Six-Day War of 1967 – has come to an end, there is nothing to stop God's plan for the world coming to its final climax.

## A place to call 'home'

What are we to make of these arguments? It goes without saying that for Israeli Jews the land is of huge significance. Herman Wouk's novel *The Hope* follows the story of an army officer and his friends as they take part in the life-and-death struggle for the birth of modern Israel from its independence in 1948 to the triumph of the Six-Day War. The Hope of the title is the State of Israel, the building of a secure homeland after the horrors of the Holocaust in which 6 million defenceless Jews were killed.

I have never known the insecurity of having no home, or the fear of an enemy coming to hunt me down. So I can hardly imagine what it felt like to be a European Jew in the 1940s, or how desperate was the Jewish longing for a land of their own. But I once met an Israeli Jew who told me, 'My father was the only one of eleven brothers in Czechoslovakia to survive the Holocaust. He escaped and made his home here. We owe everything to Israel.'

I could see in his eyes the suffering, the pride, the determination to defend Israel against all aggression. He seemed to carry within himself the tortured history of his race. I learnt from him the importance of the land for Jews today.

But if I accept the human and political significance of modern Israel, should I accept the claim that it represents fulfilled prophecy? I noticed the following advert in a Christian newspaper:

### BIBLE PROPHECIES COME TRUE

| | |
|---|---|
| Jeremiah 16:14–15 | Ingathering of Exiles |
| Isaiah 10:3 | Your help is needed |
| Romans 15:25–27 | Sharing your blessings |
| Isaiah 60:17–18 | Peace in the Holy Land |

Your investment in Israel is strength for Israel.
The seeds of peace have been planted. Help nurture
this peace by investing in State of Israel Bonds.

LET BIBLICAL PROPHECIES
GUIDE YOU IN YOUR ENDEAVOURS

STATE OF ISRAEL BONDS

I understand that a Bible-loving Jew might warm to this invitation. But how should a Christian respond? First, what about the promise of the land to Abraham's descendants and the prophecies of return after exile?

## Already fulfilled

Most of the promises about scattered Israel being brought back to the land were addressed to Jews transferred by force to Babylon after the destruction of Jerusalem in 586 BC. They promise a return to the land after a period of exile. And they *were* fulfilled when in 539 BC Cyrus the Persian, recent conqueror of Babylon, issued a decree that captive peoples could return to their own lands.

Ezekiel, for example, interpreted his vision of dry bones brought back to life as a picture of Israel restored:

> They say, 'Our bones are dried up and our hope is gone; we are cut off' . . . This is what the Sovereign LORD says: O my people, I am going to open your graves and bring you up from them; I will bring you back to the land of Israel.     (Ezekiel 37:11–12)

There is no reason to think that such prophecies – or those cited by State of Israel Bonds – waited to be fulfilled in the twentieth century. People may point out that the prophets sometimes promise a return 'from among the nations'. Since Babylon was only one nation, must this not refer to a different, later return to the land? To them I say that the prophets themselves made no such tidy distinction. In a single passage of Jeremiah, for example, God said:

> I will surely save you out of a distant place . . .
> I [will] completely destroy all the nations
>      among which I scatter you.
>
> (Jeremiah 30:10–11)

To drive a wedge between these references to '*a* place' and '*all* the nations' is to adopt a literalism which is foreign to the prophets' way of speaking.

Another approach is to point out that the vivid prophecies of Jews returning to the land to enjoy security and prosperity were only *partly* fulfilled by the return from Babylon. The experience of the returned exiles was that they were still subjects of the Persian empire. The land remained poor and precarious. Should we not say that the *real* fulfilment remained in the future – and that we find it in the existence and the growing prosperity of the State of Israel?

It is true that biblical prophecies sometimes find both an immediate fulfilment and a larger fulfilment at a later time. The prophecy in Isaiah 7:14 that 'the virgin will conceive' had an immediate reference in Isaiah's own time, but Matthew reapplied it to the birth of Jesus (Matthew 1:22–23). But let's look at what the New Testament actually does with one of these prophecies of a restored Israel.

## Surprising fulfilment

At a meeting in Jerusalem, probably in AD 49, Christian leaders debated whether Paul and others were right to welcome non-Jews into the church without requiring their men to be circumcised. James, leader of the Jerusalem church, approved of Paul's attitude and quoted Amos's prophecy in support:

> After this I will return
>    and rebuild David's fallen tent.
> Its ruins I will rebuild,
>    and I will restore it,
> that the remnant of humanity may seek the Lord,
>    and all the Gentiles who bear my name.
>                    (Acts 15:16–17,
>                referring to Amos 9:11–12)

Amos was referring to the rebuilding of the nation of Israel and the welcoming of Gentiles into it. James said this prophecy was being fulfilled as Gentiles came into the church of Jesus! And the other apostles present evidently agreed.

An original promise of restoration for Israel's political fortunes found its fulfilment in the remaking of God's people as a community of both Jews and Gentiles gathered around Jesus the Messiah. This doesn't mean that the original promise has been abandoned. But the stakes have been raised. In line with the ancient promise to Abraham that through his descendants the Gentiles would find blessing, Israel is no longer defined merely racially or geographically. The people of God is defined as those – Jews and Gentiles – who are committed to Jesus as God's Messiah.

Nowhere in fact does Jesus or any New Testament writer support the hope of a political future for Israel. This doesn't of course mean that there would never again be a state called Israel, or that God would have no purpose for such a state. It does mean that Christians should be cautious about regarding that state as the specific fulfilment of prophecy or as the sure sign that Christ's coming is just round the corner.

## The Middle East today

This means that, from a Christian perspective, disputes about territorial and human rights in the Middle East today can't be settled by simple appeal to biblical promises and predictions. Christians have sometimes given the impression that they support the State of Israel, however it behaves, just because – in their view – its existence is a fulfilment of prophecy.

But here we have to note another aspect of biblical prophecy: it is frequently conditional. That means that it's never simply a matter of saying, 'Watch the predicted event coming; there's nothing you can do to change it.' The course of history is not fixed, like a game of chess programmed by computer. History involves human choices, including our reactions to God. Yes, God promised the land to Abraham's descendants for ever – a mark of his love and total commitment to his people. But he also said: 'You must keep my covenant, you and your descendants' (Genesis 17:8–9).

So, even without the new perspective which Jesus and the New Testament bring, we would have to say that there are no unconditional guarantees of Israel's right to the land. God's people have always lived under his word of judgment as well as his word of extravagant generosity. The Israel of any particular period could be threatened with rejection, and could actually experience defeat and exile.

The prophets not only speak about the future, they speak about how the future is affected by human justice and injustice. Jeremiah warned the people of Jerusalem:

> If you do not oppress the alien, the fatherless or the widow and do not shed innocent blood in this place, and if you do not follow other gods to your own harm, then I will let you live in this place, in the land I gave to your ancestors for ever and ever. (Jeremiah 7:6–7)

Even though the land was given 'for ever', it could be lost by persistent injustice. The exile followed within a few years of Jeremiah's warning. And Israel today can't hide behind claims of 'a biblical right to the land' while injustice is practised in its name. The torture of prisoners, artillery attacks on innocent civilians, the beating of Boy Scouts in a Palm Sunday procession and the confiscation of land are acts of injustice whether committed by Israel or any other state.

Rabbi John Rayner argues that their millennia-old link

with the land and their need for security from persecution give Jews a powerful claim on the land. But, he says, the presence for centuries of Palestinian Arabs in the land gives them a claim also. So a way of sharing it must be found. The basis for this conclusion is not merely political. It springs from the conviction that God cares for all people and demands of them justice, compassion and peace. And this God 'expects the Jewish people not only to pursue its own self-interest but to be "a light to the nations" (Isaiah 49:6)'.

## Ten Lost Tribes

One further point about the prophecies of return to the land concerns the Ten Lost Tribes. The Jews who went into exile in Babylon in 586 BC comprised the two tribes of the southern kingdom, Judah, whose capital was Jerusalem. But the other ten tribes belonged to the northern kingdom of Israel, exiled to Assyria in 722 BC. They were scattered across the vast Assyrian empire and never returned to Palestine.

Now some of the prophecies of return from exile speak of all twelve tribes taking part in the resettlement of the land. For example, the vision of the dry bones brought back to life in Ezekiel 37 is interpreted there as pointing to the restoration of all twelve tribes in a united nation. And so it is argued that, since the return to the land in 539 BC involved only the two tribes of the southern kingdom, the fulfilment of Ezekiel's prophecy remains in the future.

There has been speculation throughout history as to where the ten tribes have got to, and how they might one day return to the land of promise. Do they, perhaps, include the Durani people of Afghanistan, who call themselves the Children of Israel and observe customs such as circumcision and Jewish dietary laws? There are tribal groups who keep some Jewish customs also in India, China and several parts of Africa. Some of the Ethiopian Jews who returned to Israel in the 1980s claim descent from the northern tribe of Dan. Will more groups like this make their way to Israel in order to bring the prophecies to their fulfilment?

Such speculation has its attractions. But it isn't supported by Scripture itself. Parts of the Bible written after the return from exile describe the nation restored from Babylon as embodying God's purpose for the *whole* nation, the *whole* people of God. When they rebuilt and rededicated the temple in Jerusalem they sacrificed animals 'for all Israel, twelve male goats, one for each of the tribes of Israel' (Ezra 6:17). And Paul saw himself as part of a race of twelve tribes, not two (Acts 26:7). So, from a biblical viewpoint, we're not still looking for a future fulfilment of these promises. There's already a past fulfilment.

## Figment of the imagination?

Where does the fig tree fit into all this? Just because in the Bible the fig tree sometimes alludes to Israel, we shouldn't assume that it does so in Mark 13. When Jesus took familiar pictures from life, such as harvest or sheep or parties, he used them in various ways according to the need of the moment. In Mark 13:28–30, as we suggested in chapter 5, he saw the sprouting of the fig tree's leaves (first-century troubles) as a sign that summer (the destruction of Jerusalem) was near. This offers no help to today's date-fixers.

It's certainly tempting to see Luke 21:24 – 'Jerusalem will be trampled on by the Gentiles until the times of the Gentiles are fulfilled' – as pointing to the establishment of Israel in 1948, or the recapture of the Old City of Jerusalem in 1967. But the meaning isn't so clear. 'The times of the Gentiles', like 'a time, times and half a time' in Daniel 7:25, points to a limited period during which Israel suffers at the hands of Gentile oppressors. But Jesus does not say here that Jewish political sovereignty will be restored when that period is ended. He leaves open what may happen, and gives no firm ground for conclusions about the end of history.

## God's care for Israel

So the New Testament makes no promises about a political future for Israel. But it certainly makes promises about God's continuing care and future plans for Israel as a *people*. In Romans 9 – 11 Paul agonizes over Jews who have not believed in Jesus. If he is the Messiah whom God had promised to the Jews, why have so few Jews responded to him?

His conclusion is that in God's providence Jewish resistance to the Christian message has meant that non-Jews are getting their opportunity to find new life in Christ. And in God's good time, the Gentiles' experience of all that God gives to them through Christ will provoke Jews to see what they are missing. For the time being, Gentiles are like wild olive shoots grafted into the cultivated olive tree which is Israel. But the time is coming when the natural branches will be grafted back in again.

In this way, Paul writes, 'all Israel will be saved' (Romans 11:26). He can hardly mean that every individual Jew will find salvation, since he always insists that we can enter into relationship with God only through faith in him. 'Everyone who calls on the name of the Lord will be saved' (Romans 10:13). But he clearly expects a large number of Jews to turn to Jesus the Messiah. And this great vision keeps him going when Jewish believers in Jesus are few, and drives him on to share the good news with all who are ready to hear it.

There have been times in history when significant numbers of Jews have become believers in Jesus. And this is true in many parts of the world today. The singer Helen Shapiro was 'hit between the eyes' by prophecies about the Messiah in the Hebrew Scriptures. She had seen various quotes on Christmas cards, such as the promise in Isaiah 9: 'For to us a child is born, to us a son is given . . .'

'But', she writes, 'I'd always thought they came from the New Testament. Now I realized that it was in Isaiah 9:6. One of ours!'

This was part of her journey of discovery, a journey towards the Messiah whom God had promised to her people.

One of the dangers with the kind of biblical interpretation which I criticized in chapter 5 is that it can give the impression that the Jewish people are useful only as a means of fulfilling these 'prophetic schemes'. It's as though we don't mind Israel being devastated by war because that will hasten the Lord's coming. I've even heard people criticizing the Middle East peace process because to make peace between Israel and Arab nations would hold back the predicted events which must happen before the End. That isn't Paul's position. He knows that God cares for the Jewish people for their own sake.

He makes it quite clear, then, that God hasn't finished with Israel. The God who started with Abraham to set in place his plan for the world's rescue remains committed to the care of Abraham's descendants. But he doesn't deal with the Jewish race in a way different from his dealings with other men and women. Paul's whole argument in the letter to the Romans is that 'there is no difference between Jew and Gentile' (Romans 10:12). There is one Lord of all, one gospel for all, one way of coming to know God through faith.

# One Messiah

And there is one Messiah for all. This is a hard thing to say. Isn't it arrogant for Christians to say to Jews, 'You are missing the heart of your faith. The Messiah for whom you're waiting has already come, and his name is Jesus'? Aren't we disqualified from saying such things by centuries of Christian persecution of Jews? Didn't Hitler think he was speaking for 'Christian civilization' when he wrote in *Mein Kampf*: 'By warding off the Jews I am fighting for the Lord's work'?

Yet to give up on Christian witness to Jews would be to saw off the branch on which we are sitting. Christian faith rests on the conviction that Jesus came to be the Messiah promised to Israel. Affirm that Jesus is the Messiah, and you are inevitably committed to sharing that faith with Jews whose Messiah he came to be. Deny that he is the Messiah, and there is no more reason for Christianity to exist. If Jesus is not the Messiah of the Jews, he cannot be my Saviour or the Saviour of the world.

Christians are unlikely to find the love and humility needed to speak about Jesus to Jews unless we rediscover the debt which we owe to Jews. Christianity isn't a Gentile faith. It isn't a religion different from Judaism. It's what happens when 'the God of Abraham and Isaac and Jacob' comes in the person of Jesus the Jew to open the way for Gentiles as well as Jews to receive his life. We worship a Jewish Jesus, we read a Jewish Bible. Like children who 'owe everything' to wise and generous parents, we owe a debt of gratitude to Jews, into whose inheritance we have entered.

# THE CHRIST WHO REIGNS

In a battle scene in Coppola's film *Apocalypse Now*, a messenger arrives at the front lines, looks around at the mayhem and asks, 'Who's in charge here?' No-one answers.

The same question haunts us as we look at the world. Who's in charge? Where does the power lie – in Washington or Beijing, or the headquarters of Shell or Mitsubishi? Is there anyone controlling the huge political and economic forces which battle for supremacy? Who's in charge? And we wonder whether anyone answers.

The book of Revelation is concerned with that question. To understand it properly we should ask what John, the author, claims for his book.

## Apocalypse, prophecy, letter

First, it's 'the revelation of Jesus Christ' (1:1). This word 'revelation' or 'apocalypse' hints that the book falls within the tradition of 'apocalyptic' literature', a type of literature strange to us but familiar to John and his contemporaries.

Its use of significant numbers and of weird symbols – the lamb, locusts, the dragon, for instance – would convey meaning to them, just as we readily recognize that the Magpies or the Bulls are our local football team. Ignore this apocalyptic tradition, and your interpretation is likely to be wrong-headed.

A special feature of an apocalypse is that through a series of visions it offers a new way of looking at the world. Imagine that you lived at the time when people were discovering that the world was round rather than flat. What a revolution it would bring to your understanding of navigation, geography, God, the universe and everything! Or imagine that you are lost in the maze at Hampton Court. You are surrounded by hedges and you can't see over the top. But there is someone whose job it is to climb a ladder from where he can see you and guide you out of the maze. The book of Revelation is offering a new perspective, from which all experience can be seen in a different light.

In chapters 4 and 5, John invites his readers to come with him and take a glimpse into heaven. 'I know you are surrounded by difficulties,' he says. 'If you look with me into heaven you can see God ruling. And you can see Christ, who was crucified and was raised from death for you. He isn't remote from your struggle, because he knows it from the inside. If you're aware of that heavenly perspective it can transform your understanding of the world and of your situation in it.'

Secondly, the book is prophecy (1:3). Like Old Testament prophets, John's prophecy discerns what God is doing in the contemporary situation. It stresses how the present situation must change if God's kingdom is to come. It expresses God's warnings of judgment and promises of deliverance.

Thirdly, it's a letter (1:4). Not just chapters 2 and 3 – the letters to the seven churches — but the whole book is a letter. Like any other letter, it's addressed to particular people known to the author, who must have expected them to make sense of it. He knew each of these churches in western Turkey intimately. And he knew what they might be facing, because he himself was imprisoned on the island of Patmos because of his Christian witness.

The date was probably during the AD 90s, when the Roman emperor Domitian was becoming more and more oppressive. There's little evidence that he engaged in organized persecution of Christians. But when he demanded that his subjects call him 'Lord and God', there was good reason to fear how things might develop. In Turkey itself the Christians found themselves increasingly rebuffed both by Jews and by their pagan neighbours.

And they were confronted daily by the powerful images of Rome's all-conquering vision for the world. Architecture, statues of gods and leaders, festivals in honour of Rome all proclaimed the greatness of Rome. All around these cities were inscriptions reinforcing Roman authority.

The effect was like the effect of advertising on us. We may shrug it off, and yet we are assaulted by its messages. We know that Levi jeans can be worn anywhere and that Coke will guarantee a good time. We are persuaded that 'we owe it to ourselves and to our children' to buy the latest multimedia computer. We are sure that our sexual prowess is enhanced by the right aftershave. We say we're not influenced by adverts, and then, when looking for shampoo in the supermarket, we find in our hands the brand we saw on TV last night. So, in ways we hardly notice, our values are shaped by the world around us.

# Get the picture

I settled into my seat in the cinema. I was well supplied with popcorn and was looking forward to an evening of escapism. The film was one of those blockbusters which all my friends had seen but had somehow passed me by. Until now. The lights went down, the soundtrack blasted my eardrums and my journey into the unknown began. After ten minutes the film stopped. A man stood up at the front and announced, 'That's the first section, ladies and gentlemen, so now let's take a few minutes to think about it.' And after twenty minutes of embarrassment the film continued for a few more minutes . . .

I'm only kidding. It didn't happen like that, and any cinema which operated in this way would soon be up for sale. But that's how we normally read the Bible, and we rarely stop to think how odd it is. Remember how the book of Revelation must originally have been received. The messenger went round each of the seven cities in turn, the church gathered for worship, and he read it to them from start to finish. So, like a film or a piece of music, it made its impact by the total effect of the whole thing communicated at one go.

If you try to pull apart each bit of film as you go along, you lose the story. If you try to analyse every note of a piece of music, you don't hear the tune. So when we read Revelation we shouldn't get bogged down in the details. We should let the overall thrust of its visions make their impact on us.

Of course, if you see a film or hear a symphony for the eighth time, you notice things which you didn't notice the first time. You discover depths of meaning which you never imagined before. So it's right to study Revelation carefully later, to find depths of meaning and echoes of the Old Testament which we couldn't see at first. But our danger is that we never see the thing as a whole. We never expose ourselves to its overall emotional impact and sense its grand vision. So look for the key themes. We can highlight four.

## The cross at the centre

First, John's Revelation presents the crucified Jesus as the clue to God's purpose in history. Human experience does not depend on cold fate or on meaningless chance. At the centre of history is Jesus, who, by his death, opened the way to life and showed that God is involved in the sufferings of the world. In chapter 5 Jesus is portrayed in language borrowed from the Jewish practice of sacrificing a lamb in order to experience God's forgiveness. Jesus the Lamb alone is worthy to open the scroll of human destiny and put its contents into effect.

> You are worthy to take the scroll
>     and to open its seals,
> because you were slain,
>     and with your blood you purchased for God
> members of every tribe and language and people
>         and nation.
>                                         (Revelation 5:9)

Though human rulers flex their muscles in displays of power, Jesus is 'ruler of the kings of the earth' (Revelation 1:5). But he established his rule not by force of arms, but by vulnerable, self-giving love. John's vision dares you to believe that the heavenly perspective of Revelation 5 is a truer view of how the world is meant to be than the power games you see all round you. He dares you to believe that this view will ultimately triumph.

# Evil's true colours

Secondly, Revelation exposes the nature of evil. It is embodied with terrifying force in the operations of the all-powerful state. Two symbols express the twin aspects of this sinister control over people's lives: the Beast and the Prostitute.

The Beast (chapter 13) represents political tyranny:

> People . . . worshipped the beast and asked, 'Who is like the beast? Who can make war against him?' . . . He was given power to make war against the saints and to conquer them. And he was given authority over every tribe, people, language and nation. (13:4–7)

The Prostitute (chapter 17) represents economic control, which Rome exercised through its domination of trade on the waters of the Mediterranean.

> I will show you the punishment of the great prostitute, who sits on many waters. With her the kings of the earth committed adultery and the inhabitants of the earth were intoxicated with the wine of her adulteries. (17:1–2)

The Rome of John's day embodied both political dictatorship and economic control. But they have a long history, both before then and since. And they succeed because they make evil attractive. By imposing order on chaos, political tyranny seems to promise security. That's how Hitler, and numerous twentieth-century dictators, came to power.

The fact that John described the Beast in terms of Rome's emperors in his own time should steer us away from false interpretations. The Beast is not simply the Antichrist who will appear during some future, maybe imminent, tribulation.

He represents the misuse of power over people whenever it may occur, and he is to be resisted in all his forms.

His number, 666, is no great mystery (Revelation 13:18). In Greek, Latin and Hebrew, numbers were represented by letters of the alphabet, and so it was possible to 'add up' the letters of someone's name to give a coded description. The name Nero Caesar, if written in Hebrew letters, adds up to 666. This notorious emperor was the first great persecutor of Christians. And rumours persisted, even thirty years later in Domitian's time, that he had never really died and was coming back to terrorize the Roman world. So he was a fitting symbol of all that is evil in a totalitarian state.

Worry about the actual number 666 appearing on bank cards and computer records, and about the literal stamping of numbers on people, is beside the point. What *should* concern us is the way in which a state, or any large organization, can use data to control and manipulate. Bureaucracies become impersonal instruments of control which make ordinary people powerless.

I remember a school principal wanting to discuss with the education authority a decision which he felt was having a harmful effect on the school. He phoned the authority but could get no-one to discuss it. So he went to the offices and demanded to see the person responsible. No-one owned up to having anything to do with the issue. A decision had been made and no-one was responsible for it.

Economic progress has all the imagined attractiveness of a prostitute. But the attractiveness is an illusion. Such power over people keeps them away from the truth, defies God and oppresses his people. And, as John points out, economic success tends to be built on trade not only in gold and silver, marble, rare spices, wheat and cattle. It is built on trade in human beings – people exploited as economic units, as mere commodities (Revelation 18:13). He knew how the slave system worked. And he would probably say the same today wherever prosperity is built on exploitation of cheap labour and dangerous working conditions.

## God's intentions

Revelation shows, thirdly, where God's plans are leading. They are building up to judgment on those who follow the Beast rather than the Lamb (chapters 6 – 20). This central section of the book isn't just a long-drawn-out catalogue of nasty things which God will unleash upon the world. There are three sequences, each with seven items: seven seals (Revelation 6:1 – 8:1), seven trumpets (8:2 – 11:19) and seven bowls of God's wrath (15:1 – 16:21).

These are three pictures of the same period of human history, not accounts of three periods following one after the other. Each group of seven includes reference to war and oppression, natural disaster, persecution of God's people, and the triumph of Christ. They are very like Jesus' predictions in Mark 13, and portray what may happen throughout the period from Christ's first coming to his final coming. Why do they take up so much space? Not because John takes delight in suggesting that God pours apparently endless judgments on the world, but because he recognizes how the power of evil is all-pervasive and is not easily rooted out.

Another element of God's plan is that he will show his commitment to those who remain faithful through suffering. He may not save them from persecution or even martyrdom. But he will see them through to victory (Revelation 6:9–11).

God's plan will culminate in the new creation in which everything will be set right, and God and the Lamb will be the focus of true worship (chapters 21 – 22).

# What is the church for?

The fourth theme in Revelation is the role of the church – to suffer and to witness. In chapter 11, for example, the church's role as witness to God's truth is represented by two prophetic figures. But the very act of witness provokes persecution (Revelation 11:7), so that the witnesses are called to suffering which mirrors that of their Lord. Thus Christians under an oppressive régime have a responsibility to speak the truth about Jesus and about the evil around them. And they must be ready to accept the suffering which may follow.

That is what many Christians did in South Africa during the long years of apartheid. Powerless people held hands together against oppression. How did they do it? Among other things, they sang, as negroes on American plantations and civil-rights marchers in America had sung. Listen to Allan Boesak in his book *Comfort and Protest* (1986):

> On a Sunday afternoon young black Christians [sing] as they dance around a police vehicle just after a student has been arrested at our church service.
>
> > *'It is broken, the power of Satan is broken!*
> > *We have disappointed Satan, his power is broken.*
> > *Alleluia!'*
>
> As we sing, the song is picked up by others. The police, somewhat confused, somewhat bewildered, somewhat scared, release our friend. Others join us as we march, singing and dancing, back into the church. This is a new song, a freedom song, and the power of it, the sheer joy of it, the amazing truth in it captivate and inspire thousands upon thousands throughout South Africa.

Who ever thought that music and dancing by a bunch of defenceless people, the underclass of society, would overthrow the strongholds of a police state? It's no accident that John scatters songs throughout his book. These songs express a truer vision of reality, before which all false visions, however powerful, must one day fall. And even if you see no change in the régime, even if you are threatened with arrest and even martyrdom, he says, you are called to witness to this truer vision. That is the pattern set by Jesus, the slaughtered Lamb, the 'faithful witness' (Revelation 1:5), and there is no higher calling than to follow him.

Revelation, then, isn't a detailed prediction of specific events to be unfolded at the end of history. It isn't the wild fantasies of a sectarian Christian who has opted out of society because life is too difficult and the opposition too strong. It's the vision of a man who is convinced that, like Jesus, Christians are called upon to engage with the mess and the distorted values of the world and to show how the only hope for the world's transformation lies in the upside-down values of the crucified Jesus.

## Getting the message

Revelation has always come to life for Christians facing persecution. The Japanese knew what they were doing when, during their occupation of Korea in the Second World War, they banned Korean preachers from preaching from this book.

So we shall hear its message if we listen to it alongside people on the underside of history, who live out its call to witness and to suffer when nothing else is possible: people like Allan Boesak and his colleagues in South Africa, and peasants in Latin America for whom Revelation unmasks the economic injustice under which they live and empowers them to continue the struggle.

But Revelation is written not only for people experiencing open hostility to their faith. This struck me with new force when I studied once again the message to the church in Laodicea (Revelation 3:14–22). There, after messages to six other churches which were mostly suffering persecution, the final message reveals a church which is not oppressed but comfortable, which claims to be rich and to need nothing.

This church's problem is not that it is oppressed by the surrounding culture, but that it has absorbed the culture into itself. It has avoided confrontation with Rome's alien values by making those values its own. It is barely distinguishable from its surroundings. It shows no sympathy for the other suffering churches of Asia, which it must have known about, but remains smugly content with its place in the world.

> You say, 'I am rich; I have acquired wealth and do not need a thing.' But you do not realise that you are wretched, pitiful, poor, blind and naked. (Revelation 3:17)

## Serving two masters

This all goes to show that the most serious threat to the church is not the pressure of suffering but the pressure to conform to our surrounding culture. It is possible for Christians to find themselves worshipping the Beast rather than the Lamb. Does any book of Scripture show more starkly, or with more challenge, how possible – and dangerous – it is to settle for 'serving two masters', whether they be God and money, God and the state, God and earthly security, or God and . . .?

So part of the witness to which the book of Revelation calls us is to stand firm against the values, particularly economic values, which increasingly drive our society, just as they drove the Roman state.

An Anglican clergyman whom I know attended a seminar addressed by a business consultant from America. He was a guru of 'downsizing', and his recipe for making a business more successful went like this: sack half the workforce, give the rest a big pay increase and expect twice as much work from them.

My friend stood up and asked: 'How do you see your responsibility to those made redundant?'

The guru replied: 'I have no responsibility to them – my responsibility is to the company and the shareholders.'

'But you do have a responsibility,' my friend replied. 'We are all members of society and we have responsibilities towards each other.'

Seeing his dog-collar, the guru responded, 'You would say that, wouldn't you?'

But my friend had made his witness for Christian values; he had stood out against the prevailing philosophy, and others present were grateful.

This is why John's vision of God as creator and Jesus as saviour and ruler of all the earth is so vital. When he is removed from the centre of our vision, then something else becomes dominant and ultimately enslaves us – money, the state, a political ideology, self-indulgence . . .

## Home or away?

We miss the whole point of Revelation if we take its image of the Beast (its depiction of evil) and pin it on something 'out there'. This has so often been done by people declaring that the Beast is the pope, or Stalin, or Saddam Hussein. The Beast may be closer to home. As John knows, it works its own magic on us, seducing us by its offer of prosperity and security. An American writer named William Stringfellow wrote a book on Revelation called *An Ethic for Christians and Other Aliens in a Strange Land* (1973). He argued that the beast was not some external force. It was the way in which the American state and all the goals and values which supported it were controlling people's assumptions about what they should aim for and how they should behave. 'The task is to treat the nation within the tradition of biblical politics – to understand America biblically – not the other way round, not . . . to construe the Bible Americanly.'

This isn't just an American problem. We are all inclined to read the Bible through the filters of our own society. If, for example, our society generally accepts widespread abortion, or male domination, or a widening gap between rich and poor, we shall mostly filter out those parts of the Bible which challenge such assumptions. That's why we need the stark message of Revelation, to confront our skill at compromise.

## Realistic vision

John's is a realistic vision. He knows the weakness of the churches, as he makes clear in the messages to the seven churches (chapters 2 – 3). Yet he believes that God can sustain them. He knows the power and glory of Rome, yet sees in it the evil of totalitarian force and the deceptiveness of economic prosperity. He knows how great are the forces of evil which ravage the earth, but he has a clear picture of the ultimate triumph of the cross of Jesus. He shows how God's ultimate victory, and little victories along the way, are won not by force, but by the power of vulnerable love displayed in the crucified Jesus.

In 1989, churches in Czechoslovakia were permitted for the first time for forty years to put a notice board outside their buildings. The leaders of a little Methodist church in Prague met to consider what they should write on their notice board. Should it be the minister's name and phone number? The times of services? They wrote simply: 'THE LAMB WINS.'

# BEYOND DEATH'S DOOR

Bill was an unusual friend. He was always probing issues, asking questions no-one else dared ask. He was totally unconventional – a loner, you might have thought. Yet he had an enormous capacity for friendship. He had a mind sharp as a rapier and a heart full of compassion. And he was a writer of distinction, with two or three books published and many more inside him.

He and a friend were travelling to research their next book when they died in a plane crash in Nepal. Bill was thirty-three. What a waste, I thought as I tried to absorb the news. Why him? My mind was a confusion of anger and sadness, and regret that I had not seen more of him in recent years. Yet at the thanksgiving service we were able to sing with feeling:

> Thine be the glory, risen, conquering Son,
> Endless is the victory thou o'er death hast won.

Our grief at the loss of a friend was tempered by a deeper

truth – that Jesus Christ has conquered death and God holds our dead friend in his care.

## Death and taxes

It was Benjamin Franklin who said, 'In this world nothing can be said to be certain except death and taxes.' Taxes we learn to live with, but death is more of a problem. Another person's death is unwelcome because it leaves things unfinished, and the bereaved are left behind to pick up the pieces. And the prospect of our own death is disturbing because it's a lonely journey into the unknown. 'I'm scared of no-one. I'm only scared of death,' Muhammad Ali, heavyweight boxing champion of the world, once said. 'Everybody wants to go to heaven but nobody wants to die.'

People react to this prospect in a variety of ways. Some just shrug their shoulders. Actor Dudley Moore said: 'I worry about dying and am waiting for the first physical ailment to hit. There's nothing to save us. I don't believe in God or an afterlife. I'll just sell my house and pay out whatever I have left in hospital bills. That's what lies in wait for us. But I'm quite content. I'm OK. I don't know what else one can hope for.'

The prospect of death spurs others to focus their lives on worthwhile goals and to appreciate life with a heightened sense of wonder. Anita Roddick, founder of The Body Shop and campaigner on green issues, confided in a radio interview that she is driven by fear of death. She meant that we have only one life, and there is nothing beyond it. We have only one brief spell in which to make our mark, to make a lasting contribution to the world.

# Lettuce and vitamin pills

Other people are into the business of defying death. And it *is* big business. Miller Quarles is a Texas millionaire and holder of the Houston over-80s tennis title. He has set up a company to research how human body cells can be made to multiply in a way which will guarantee the constant renewal of the body. Unfortunately his chief research scientist has got diverted into seeking a cure for cancer. So Quarles keeps healthy on lettuce leaves, mineral water and a cocktail of vitamin pills, hoping to get the research back on track before it's too late for him.

Most younger people don't have the same concern. Death, they feel, is a long way off. They may have watched 20,000 deaths on TV before they were old enough to vote. But death isn't real. It's something that happens to other people. And they may get beyond middle age before they see a dead body. They are certainly unlikely to witness anyone dying at home. In Britain and the United States four-fifths of all deaths take place in hospital.

So death becomes remote, something we don't know how to talk about. It's strange, then, that while even Christians struggle to talk about death and what lies beyond, a number of films have invited us to reflect on it. In *Ghosts*, Demi Moore's mourning for her murdered lover is softened by his spooky reappearance to pursue his killers and reassure her. In *Truly, Madly, Deeply* Juliet Stevenson is surprised by the reappearance of her dead lover. In *Dead Again*, Kenneth Branagh and Emma Thompson discover they have been lovers in a previous existence. The questions simply won't lie down.

# What's the evidence?

Death is real. Death is disturbing. Death is conquered. That is the Christian conviction. But why believe it? Might it be a piece of wishful thinking – we can't cope with our mortality so we project our hopes into a future fantasy? Did we invent belief in life after death as a way of compensating for the present life being too short, too miserable or too unfair?

Christians have three grounds for confidence in a life beyond death. First, we know something about God's love. God has shown us through Jesus how much he loves the people he has created. He has made us to know him – nothing less. How could we believe that God will abandon us to nothingness? The Father of Jesus Christ isn't like that.

God offers us a second reason for confidence. He raised Jesus from death, 'the guarantee that those who sleep in death will also be raised' (1 Corinthians 15:20, GNB). If we live in relationship to him, we share in his resurrection. John's gospel tells how Jesus responded to the grief of two sisters at the death of their brother.

> I am the resurrection and the life. Those who believe in me will live even though they die, and whoever lives and believes in me will never die. Do you believe this?     (John 11:25–26)

And he restored the dead man to life, as a sign of his own coming victory over death and its significance for all people.

The third ground of hope is the Christian's present experience of God's love and power. We hope for life beyond death not merely to compensate for what we don't have now, but so that we may experience in full what we already experience in part. Listen to Paul:

The one who raised the Lord Jesus from the dead will also raise us with Jesus and present us with you in his presence . . . Therefore we do not lose heart. Though outwardly we are wasting away, yet inwardly we are being renewed day by day.

(2 Corinthians 4:14, 16)

In the same vein, New Testament writers speak of 'eternal life' not as something we get after death, but as something to be experienced *now*. 'Those who believe in the Son *have* eternal life' and '*have crossed over* from death to life' (John 3:36; 5:24). Eternal life is a quality of relationship to God which is experienced through faith in Jesus now. Whatever happens beyond death is a development of present experience.

## The significance of resurrection

But what form does life after death take? 'I don't mind dying,' a friend commented to me, 'but I have no clear hope about what happens afterwards.' What could I say to him? In the supermarket of ideas various options are on display. Some people favour reincarnation, the belief that death leads to rebirth in another body. As many as a quarter of Europeans and Americans claim to be attracted to it.

But the idea raises far more questions than it solves. What kind of justice is there in a system where my position in life is fixed by behaviour in a previous life, even though I have no means of knowing what it was I did wrong? And if, as some gurus of reincarnation claim, I can choose what my future reincarnations will be, where does that leave the free will of those future lives I will inhabit? The biblical message is that 'it is appointed to mortals to die *once*, and after that comes judgement' (Hebrews 9:27, NRSV).

Another belief is that at death we are re-absorbed into a life

force or into the eternal One, losing our individual conscious-
ness like a drop of water falling in the ocean. But that hardly
sounds like a destiny to be hoped for.

More familiar in the western world is the view that the soul
is immortal by nature, and at death will be released from the
body to enjoy a higher life in heaven. But the origins of this
theory are Greek rather than biblical. It tends to regard
immortality as ours by right, rather than as a gift of God. And
it encourages the notion that life after death is a rather pale
reflection of the full-bodied existence of earthly life.

But the New Testament speaks normally of *resurrection*. 'By
his power God raised the Lord from the dead, and he will raise
us also' (1 Corinthians 6:14). God intends to raise from death
all who are united to Christ, just as Christ himself was raised.

To say that God raises us up, or that we are resurrected,
means that our future life depends on God's power, not on
some power within ourselves. It stresses that eternal life is
God's gift, not our achievement. God the creator is in the
business of new creation. Whereas reincarnation denies the
reality of death, resurrection conquers it.

## Body language

Resurrection language implies that the whole person is raised
to life, not merely some part of us, the soul. Christ, says Paul,
'will transform our lowly bodies so that they will be like his
glorious body' (Philippians 3:21). The resurrection body of
Jesus is the designer's pattern for the resurrection of his
followers. After Jesus rose from death he was no mere ghostly
figure, nor was he simply a physical body returned to life. His
body was transformed, suitable for life in a new and glorious
environment. It was different, yet still the same Jesus.

So it shall be with us. Paul says we shall have 'spiritual

bodies' – personalities energized by God's Spirit and suited to the environment of the world to come (1 Corinthians 15:44). We shall be no mere shadows of our former selves. Nor shall we be simply the old body patched up. We shall be transformed for the life of God's new world. Paul uses the image of a seed and the resulting plant to emphasize that there is a real continuity between the person who dies and the person who is raised up. He then delights in the contrast between the dying and the rising:

> The body that is sown is perishable, it is raised imperishable; it is sown in dishonour, it is raised in glory; it is sown in weakness, it is raised in power; it is sown a physical body, it is raised a spiritual body. (1 Corinthians 15:42–44)

We can't say how God does this. But we can say he has shown that he knows how to do it by raising Jesus from the grave. We can say that the God who places infinite value on every human person longs to confirm that value by raising us to be like the risen Jesus.

## When will the resurrection happen?

The New Testament links our resurrection with Jesus' final coming. For example, Paul's earliest discussion of this theme was responding to anxiety about the fate of Christians who had already died. 'Don't worry,' he said, 'when Jesus comes, those who have already died will be raised up to meet the Lord along with those who are still alive' (see 1 Thessalonians 4:13–18).

Now that raises a problem. Where are the dead now? Is it wrong to say that people go to be with Christ when they die? Paul wrote: 'I desire to depart and be with Christ.' He also wrote: 'We eagerly await a Saviour from [heaven] . . . who will transform our lowly bodies so that they will be like his glorious body' (Philippians 1:23; 3:20–21). How could he say both these things in the same letter? How could Jesus speak of a future resurrection, and yet promise the thief on the cross, '*Today* you will be with me in paradise' (Luke 23:43)?

Learned volumes have debated how we can believe at the same time that believers are with Christ immediately at death and that we wait for resurrection at Christ's coming. But perhaps they make it too complicated. For at death we pass beyond the earthly measurements of time. All who die in faith are firmly grasped by Christ's love. For them, liberated from earth's timescale, resurrection at Christ's coming is the next event. It is only those who continue in earthly life who see resurrection at Christ's coming as still a future event.

So the timing doesn't matter. What does matter is that those who die trusting in Christ are secure in his love, and that death need hold no fear for them.

## Life in tomorrow's world

If you were moving house next month you would want to know something about the district to which you were moving. And it's perfectly natural that we should ask questions about what God's new world is like. There are many questions which can't be answered, because it lies beyond our experience. But the Bible offers us a number of pictures to whet our appetite.

It speaks not so much about 'going to heaven when we die' as about 'a new heaven and a new earth' (2 Peter 3:13; Revelation 21:1). The picture is of a universe transformed, perfected – fit surroundings for God's eternal presence with his people. This encourages us to think that the next world and its surroundings will not be less real or solid than our present world, but more so. And it will involve not just human individuals but the whole of God's creation. God's plan, we recall, is 'to bring all creation together, everything in heaven and on earth, with Christ as head' (Ephesians 1:10, GNB).

In a series of pictures, Jesus promised that the upside-down world will at last be put right. Those who are last will become first, the small will become great, the poor will become rich. The lost will be found and will be at home for ever in the Father's love.

So, in contrast to our experience of the present world, God 'will wipe every tear from their eyes. There will be no more death or mourning or crying or pain, for the old order of things has passed away' (Revelation 21:4). Everything which limits human life will be taken away. Disfigured and disabled bodies will be replaced by resurrection bodies. Those whose minds have ceased to function through old age or injury will be wonderfully renewed.

A friend of mine who worked in Rwanda knew an old man for whom this hope was vivid. 'How are you, Thomas?' my friend would ask.

He would reply, 'My body is terrible, my knees are giving way, there is pain everywhere, but I praise God just because he is my Saviour.' Then he would beam with a huge smile and add, 'And I can't wait to get to heaven because I'm going to have new knees and new ankles and a new back, and I'll be able to move around and dance and praise God all day long.'

The other piece of putting right our upside-down world will be the end of all evil – the end of evil within me and the end of the evil which surrounds me. In his vision John sees the devil, the ultimate source of all temptation, thrown to destruction in the lake of fire (Revelation 20:10). Evil is banished from the universe, never to return.

The pictures Jesus uses to speak of this new world are those of a party, a home and a city.

## Welcome to the new world!

First, Jesus liked to picture God's coming reign as a *party*. God himself will be the host, people from east and west will take their seats, and there will be worship and excitement and dancing. It will be a celebration of God's triumph such as the world has never seen before (Luke 13:29; 14:15–24). Definitely an occasion not to be missed! Revelation 19 adds a further dimension by describing it as a wedding celebration, at which Christ is united for ever with the church as his bride.

Secondly, in the new heavens and new earth, *God* will be at the centre and his people will be at *home* with him.

> I heard a loud voice from the throne saying, 'Now the dwelling [the home, GNB] of God is with human beings, and he will live with them. They will be his people, and God himself will be with them and be their God.' (Revelation 21:3)

In our human experience there's nothing so satisfying and life-enhancing as to feel really 'at home' with someone we love and trust. With such a person we feel we can be completely honest, we can explore the challenges of life and we can face together anything which may come our way. To be at home with the God who made us and loves us will be the most wonderful experience we can imagine.

If we're honest, we often don't feel that God is the real centre of our lives and that we want nothing more than to be close to him. But there are moments when we feel a kind of homesickness for God's presence, a sense that he is where we really belong. We may be sure then that he's preparing us for what's to come.

This is the point at which to raise a question which sometimes surfaces in our minds. Isn't it selfish to want to go to heaven? Do we believe in Jesus because of what we're going to get out of it? The amazing news is that God wants to be with *us*. Heaven isn't a prize for being good or a product which we choose for our own selfish satisfaction. It's our real home, prepared by a loving Father. To want to be there isn't selfish any more than it is selfish for a child to want to enjoy her parents' company.

The final picture of God's new world is the *city*. 'I saw the Holy City, the new Jerusalem, coming down out of heaven from God' (Revelation 21:2). In the modern world we have mixed views about cities. They are places of life, activity, satisfying work, sports grounds, cinemas, concert halls and so much that makes life interesting and exciting. They are also places of decay, pollution, crime, unemployment, racial tension and deep loneliness.

The biblical image of the city is a positive one. It means that the new world will be a place of community. God's people will be together, in all their rich variety – 'people from every tribe, language, nation, and race' (Revelation 5:9, GNB).

This is one reason why 'resurrection bodies' are so important. It's the body that marks each of us as a unique person distinct from others. It's through our bodies that we express ourselves and communicate with others. It's through our bodies that we are recognized by others. So to speak of resurrection bodies means that we shall have all those aspects in the life to come. We shall remain distinct individuals, but we shall be in relationship to others.

Shall we recognize our loved ones? Certainly, but we shall no doubt learn to recognize others too! When Jesus said that people from all over the world would sit down with Abraham, Isaac and Jacob when God's reign finally comes, he must have assumed they would be recognized (Matthew 8:11).

## Life in the city

The image of the city suggests activity. Far from being a place of boring inactivity, the new world will be dominated by love. And love is active, creative, always developing. A lover who is living temporarily at a distance from the loved one doesn't speak of being bored at the prospect of spending unlimited time in her company! So why should we imagine that in heaven we'll run out of things to do?

This activity will include human creativity. 'The greatness and the wealth of the nations will be brought into the city' (Revelation 21:26, GNB). Because God is a creative God who declared the world good when he made it, he won't simply write it off with all its wealth of art and beauty and human inventiveness. Heaven is no world-denying nirvana, but an eternal 'yes' to the goodness of God's creation. It isn't a colourless existence, but a totally fulfilling world worthy of its Creator.

The city is a place of safety – for ever. In the world of the Bible, people thought of the city not as a wasteland of violence and loneliness, but as a place of security. Here you were safe from enemies and were free to celebrate life with your neighbours under the protection of the king.

God's promise is that tomorrow's world will be better than all that is best in today's world. And that should be assurance enough for anyone. It was enough for Dietrich Bonhoeffer, the Christian pastor executed by the Nazis in 1945. 'This is the end,' were his last words to his friends. 'For me, the beginning of life.'

# THE CHOICE IS YOURS

In her *Sylvia* cartoons, Nicole Hollander imagines hell as a place where square dancing is compulsory, cable TV is in Latin and newspapers are devoted exclusively to the love lives of film stars. In Gary Larson's *Far Side*, hell is a banal wasteland of banjo and accordion music, cold coffee and maths problems. In Joe Martin's *Mr Boffo*, hell is where the eternally condemned earn 25 cents a year at hard labour but the Coke machine takes only $10,000 bills. As we smile at the jokes, the possibility that there might be a serious side to all this slips a little further into the background.

Other factors are at work too, undermining belief in life after death. In the twentieth century, many have experienced hell on earth – in the trenches of the First World War, in the Nazi gas chambers, in Cambodia, Bosnia and Rwanda. Can anything in the next life be worse than this, we wonder. And when our image of hell owes more to the comedian and cartoonist than to the New Testament, we conclude that it cannot.

The whole idea of life after death, of heaven, hell and

judgment, has come under suspicion in modern times. We prefer not to have someone else making the rules which decide our future. We like to be independent, and the more we like it the more we become convinced that this is the way things are. It's like arriving at the customs post with a car full of taxable goods – and finding no-one there. The suspicion that this is in fact the case spreads quickly, because it is what we would all prefer to believe.

But still the questions linger. *Daily Mirror* columnist Marjorie Proops was for a time so troubled by fear of death that she consulted a psychiatrist. When someone asked if her worries arose from a sense that death is the end, she replied that her real worry was that death might *not* be the end.

We saw in the last chapter that 'it is appointed for mortals to die once, and after that comes judgement' (Hebrews 9:27, NRSV). The message that God will confront us in a final judgment is a constant theme in the Bible. And it can't be dismissed as the harsh doctrine of a half-baked follower of Jesus, for no-one spoke more forcefully of God's judgment than Jesus himself.

## Bearing responsibility

Before we dismiss it too quickly, we should reckon what happens when the idea of judgment is lost. If we are to give an account of our lives to God, that must mean that God takes all our actions seriously. The choices we make, the things we do, matter to him. No word or action is without significance. He treats us as responsible beings. That is something which distinguishes us from animals. If we abandon the belief that we shall give account of ourselves to God, we are reducing responsibility, diminishing our humanity. We are saying that in the long run nothing matters.

Many people run away from the message of God's judgment because of false ideas which have gathered around it. Let's try to express clearly what it means.

## The Judge is our Saviour

First, we shall be judged by the God made known to us in Jesus. 'We will all stand before God's judgment seat' (Romans 14:10). 'We must all appear before the judgment seat of Christ' (2 Corinthians 5:10). Paul can use either expression. It makes no difference. It makes clear that judgment is not the act of a cosmic sadist who has set obstacles in our way and delights to see us trip over them into hell. Our judge is Jesus, who has done everything to show God's love to us and to bring us into friendship with him. He has lived our life and understands our experience.

## Judgment for all

Secondly, all people will be judged. As those statements of Paul put it, we must all make our appearance before him. The living and the dead, people of all faiths and none, people of influence and people whom the world counts as nobodies – all will come under the searching gaze of our Creator and Saviour. No exception, no escape, no excuses.

## Judged on what we've done

Thirdly, we shall be judged according to our deeds. 'The Son of Man is to come with his angels in the glory of his Father', said Jesus, 'and then he will repay everyone for what has been done' (Matthew 16:27, NRSV). Nowhere is this theme more vividly portrayed than in the judgment scene where sheep are divided from goats according to what they have done for the poor, the hungry, the imprisoned, the sick and the friendless immigrant (Matthew 25:21–36). Jesus identifies with those who suffer and are in need and says: 'You show what your attitude to me is by the way you react to other women and men in their suffering. And on that reaction depends your ultimate destiny.' A poem puts it like this:

> Under our noses, before our eyes,
> Not in the clouds, not in the sky,
> He passes. And we pass him by.
> Humanity is his disguise.
> (It works too well).

But this raises the question: how can it be that we are judged according to our deeds if — as every alert reader of the New Testament knows — God accepts us and gives eternal life on the basis of our trust in him?

The two ideas aren't in fact in conflict. A person who trusts in Christ is brought into relationship with the living God and begins to experience God's power at work. This isn't something we earn or achieve. It is a gift of God's generous love. But, like any gift, it is ours only if we receive it and make use of it. The only kind of faith which God recognizes as real is what Paul calls 'faith working through love' — faith working itself out in God-inspired acts of care towards others (Galatians 5:6). At God's final judgment our deeds will reveal what kind of person we are. Our deeds — stripped of all the pretence and self-justification with which we so often clothe them — will be the evidence which shows whether our faith is real.

At the final judgment, it won't just be our outward, public deeds that come under examination. There are many who have never been found guilty of any crime, and yet inwardly are seething with destructive bitterness, hatred or sheer self-concern. All this will be revealed 'on the day when God, through Jesus Christ, will judge the secret thoughts of all' (Romans 2:16, NRSV).

Many people say, 'I'm as good as the next person', or 'I've never done anyone any harm' – as though that were an adequate defence. Here are people created to reflect God's character in the world, with so much potential for good, so many possibilities of making the world a better place. And all they can say is, 'I never did anyone any harm.'

Our deeds, our words, our thoughts, our motives and our characters will be laid bare before God. All the information will be available, and there will be no miscarriage of justice. If allowances have to be made for people's background or limited opportunities to respond to the nudgings of God's Spirit, we may trust the loving and all-knowing God to deal justly with those situations.

We aren't responsible for our background, our temperament, our natural gifts or lack of them. But we *are* responsible for our character, and the direction in which we set it shapes our future.

> Do not be deceived: God cannot be mocked. People reap what they sow. Those who sow to please their sinful nature, from that nature will reap destruction; those who sow to please the Spirit, from the Spirit will reap eternal life. (Galatians 6:7–8)

## *Judgment brings division*

Fourthly, the final judgment will be a moment of division between those who are revealed truly to belong to Christ and those who do not. In the passage about the sheep and the goats, it's expressed like this:

> The King will say to those on his right, 'Come, you who are blessed by my Father . . .' Then . . . to those on his left, 'Depart from me . . .'                     (Matthew 25:34, 41)

Another way of expressing all this is to say that the big question is whether we are in relationship to God through Christ or not. The benchmark by which we are judged is our relationship to him. Are we united with him through a faith which works itself out in practice? Or are we among those who 'do not know God and do not obey the gospel of our Lord Jesus' (2 Thessalonians 1:8)?

The outcome of the judgment also is a matter of relationship. While a positive verdict leads to being 'with the Lord for ever' (1 Thessalonians 4:17), a negative outcome is to be excluded outside in the dark (Matthew 22:13).

The language of relationship draws attention to a further point. *Judgment is taking place now and all the time.* It isn't reserved for a future occasion after our death or at Jesus' final coming. We are choosing our relationship to God as we respond to Christ or turn away from him. John's gospel puts this very plainly.

God did not send the Son into the world to condemn the world, but in order that the world might be saved through him. Those who believe in him are not condemned; but those who do not believe are condemned already, because they have not believed in the name of the only Son of God. And this is the judgement, that the light has come into the world, and people loved darkness rather than light because their deeds were evil. (John 3:17–19, NRSV)

It isn't God's desire to condemn, any more than it is the purpose of light to cast shadows. But shadows are inevitably cast when someone stands in the way of the light. We choose now our relationship with God as we respond to Jesus' offer of forgiveness and new life, and as we react to the ways he confronts us through the needs of others. The final judgment will be God's underlining of the choices we've made. If we are in relationship to God now, we shall enter into a fuller experience of his presence then. If we turn away from him now, we shall find that decision confirmed then.

## Cut off from God

'It's hell.' We've all heard the comment. It may come from someone describing a relationship which has gone badly wrong. It may be a feeling of being totally alone and without hope in the world, or of being sidelined from normal society, locked into unemployment and bad housing. Or perhaps the way someone has chased success at work so single-mindedly has led to the break-up of marriage and family.

Such experiences have complex causes. But from one angle the word 'hell' is right. These things are what happens when people turn down the invitation to live under God's reign and to share in his life. Like a man who complains to the manufacturer that his television doesn't work under water, they may wonder why life has gone wrong. But we aren't designed to live in God's world without reference to God. As societies and as individuals we suffer the consequences of choosing our own way.

Yet this state of affairs need not be final. As long as there is breath in us we can change sides. We can have our lives put together again. We can become focused on a new centre. The invitation remains open: 'Now is the time of God's favour, now is the day of salvation' (2 Corinthians 6:2).

If there are people who turn down the invitation and find themselves excluded from God's presence, what form does their destiny take? Jesus used a range of images. He said it's like arriving late and finding the door already locked. It's like being shut out in the darkness. It's like a fruit tree that is cut down and thrown on to the fire because it didn't bear good fruit. It's like fire, burning up all that is evil. It's like being lost, never to be found again. It's like arriving at a party without an invitation and hoping for special favours from the host, only to be met by his words: 'I don't recognize you. Go away.'

Christians take different views over whether biblical teaching implies that people separated from God's presence continue to exist in 'eternal torment', or simply cease to be. The traditional view takes at face value phrases like 'eternal punishment' and 'hell, where "their worm does not die, and the fire is not quenched"' (Matthew 25:46; Mark 9:48). If 'eternal life' means life without end, 'eternal punishment' must mean punishment which goes on for ever.

Others question whether the meaning is quite so straightforward. The language of destruction suggests that people cease consciously to exist, not that they suffer torment for ever. If people cut themselves off from God, the source of all life, then the logical consequence would be that they cease to exist. 'Eternal punishment' might mean that the verdict of condemnation is unalterable, not that people suffer eternally.

The imagery which we associate with the sufferings of hell, they would add, owes more to Greek thought and medieval poetry than it does to the Bible, whose language is much more restrained. And if there were a place where people suffer for all eternity, how could that be squared with the conviction that God will one day complete his plan 'to bring all creation together . . . with Christ as head' (Ephesians 1:10, GNB)?

When this second view is aired, holders of the traditional view often retort: 'But if people merely cease to exist, what kind of punishment is that? If that were Hitler's fate, wouldn't he simply have got away with all the evil he did?' This is a real dilemma, and our instinct for justice tells us that we must not dismiss it lightly.

But there is a danger that we put the focus in the wrong place. As we saw, the heart of Jesus' message about human destiny is about relationship, or lack of relationship, to God. So the really important thing about the destiny of those who have turned away from God is that they will be separated from him. Never having loved him, they may feel that this is no great loss. But from God's point of view it is the greatest tragedy in the universe. In comparison with that, the question of precisely what form the separation might take is rather less important.

## Questions about judgment

The whole theme of God's judgment raises other questions and difficulties. Here we tackle three of them.

### *God is too merciful!*

'I believe in a God of love, who is too merciful to condemn anyone.' Anyone who has been captivated by God's love must feel the force of this argument. And yet it misunderstands the nature of love. Love never forces itself on the object of love. The moment it did so, it would cease to be love. A mother knows that her son's longing to assert his freedom is likely to lead to disaster. She warns him of the dangers, but in the end she must let him go. Her love for him means she will respect his freedom, however painful she finds it to let him go.

Similarly, it is God's respect for human freedom which makes hell possible. We know that God is patient with people because he doesn't want any to perish, but all to come to repentance (2 Peter 3:9). We don't know in how many ways and how many times he may try to win people to respond to his love. But we know that love, if it is to remain love, must take the risk of being rejected – perhaps for ever.

'That would be defeat for God,' we might say. But maybe we should call it not defeat but miracle. It *is* a miracle that God so respects the freedom of people he has made that he allows the possibility of their refusal to have anything to do with him.

## A second chance?

'But surely God will give us a second chance.' Many people hope that God will give further opportunities to turn to him after death, when the issues perhaps will be so much clearer. But God is constantly inviting us to come to him. And there's no hint in the teaching of Jesus to support the idea of further chances after death.

There is more than a hint in the opposite direction in a verse we've already looked at: 'People are destined to die once, and after that to face judgment' (Hebrews 9:27). We don't live in a fairytale world where everything will magically turn out right in the end. We live in a real world where real choices must be made. It is fantasy to believe without evidence that we shall have fresh opportunities at some future time to make choices we've been unwilling to make now.

## But some have never heard the gospel . . .

'What about those who have never heard the good news, and people of other faiths?' This is a huge issue, and there may be no tidy solution, no final answer before the judgment itself. Though some Christians may disagree with me, I would approach the question in this way.

According to Christian faith, Jesus' life, death and resurrection constitute God's special and conclusive way of bringing men and women into relationship with himself. If the love of God for the world is as Jesus portrayed it, then he couldn't be content that most of the people of his world should be condemned simply because they had no realistic opportunity to hear the Christian gospel.

Even though they insisted that Jesus is the only Saviour, the first followers of Jesus believed that people like Abraham and David, Noah and Job found acceptance with God before the time of Jesus and even outside God's special covenant with Israel. So people can be in touch with God even outside the Jewish or Christian religion. In any case, it isn't religion that saves people. If I am saved, I am saved by Christ. God does not accept me because I belong to the Christian religion any more than my Sikh friend is accepted by belonging to the Sikh religion.

Those who begin to know God without having heard the Christian message do so not because of their own insight or achievement but because God is at work in them. They are reaching out to the God who is already coming close to them. They are like Esa, who lived in Ethiopia a hundred years ago. Though he never met a preacher, he suddenly told his people that they must abandon their traditional religion and worship God the Creator. In the 1920s he died without ever hearing the good news. But thousands of his people had done what he said, and when a Christian preacher arrived in the 1930s they realized that he was filling out what they had heard from Esa. They became Christians.

Could we say that they were acceptable to God because they had heard the Christian message and responded, but that Esa was not acceptable because he didn't? I don't think so.

Yet it would be dangerous to draw general conclusions from Esa's story about how God deals with people who have not heard the Christian message clearly expressed. The one sure way to find a secure relationship with God is to put our trust in Christ and to follow in his way. That's the reason for

Paul's urgent insistence that the good news be communicated to all people:

> The same Lord is Lord of all and richly blesses all who call on him, for, 'Everyone who calls on the name of the Lord will be saved.'
>
> How, then, can they call on the one they have not believed in? And how can they believe in the one of whom they have not heard? And how can they hear without someone preaching to them? And how can they preach unless they are sent?
>
> (Romans 10:12–15)

Even if there are people like Esa who experience God's generosity without hearing the good news about Jesus, that is no reason for Christians to draw back from the task of worldwide evangelism.

Not till judgment day can there be a final answer to these questions about people who haven't heard the good news. In the meantime not all Christians will agree with me! But maybe we can agree that sensitive evangelism is more important than dogmatic debate.

## One question after another

Will there be many or few who are grasped by God's love in this way? I don't know. What I do know is that Jesus refused to answer such speculative questions. When someone asked him, 'Are only a few people going to be saved?' his reply was blunt: 'Make every effort to enter through the narrow door' (Luke 13:23–24). He wouldn't answer theoretical questions about other people, but put the question back to his hearers. The issue of human destiny isn't about Judas or Hitler or the latest international thug. It's about you and me.

The fact that Jesus puts the challenge in this way means that his invitation is still open. The best-known of all statements about God's love underlines the risk of failing to trust the God of love:

> God so loved the world that he gave his one and only Son, that whoever believes in him should not perish but have eternal life.                                                    (John 3:16)

If people persist in turning down an offer like that, who is to blame? Not God.

# WHILE THERE'S HOPE THERE'S LIFE

'While there's life there's hope,' we often say as we see people struggling with illness or the pressure of living in difficult circumstances. A deeper truth lies in putting it the other way round. As long as hope burns inside us – whatever the circumstances – we can know the life of God racing through our veins.

How, then, in the light of all we have said in the previous chapters, can we live in hope? How does the story of God's plan for the world give us a basis for hope?

## Reasons to hope

### We're loved

Hope arises from a sense of being loved. I once read a 600-page Russian novel about a man who spent his life in bed – not because he was ill, but simply because there was nothing worth getting up for. Then he fell in love, and the whole story changed. He was up and about, enjoying life with his beloved and confident about the future. He was elated by simple things like a walk in the garden and the smell of roses. But the love affair came to an end, and he went back to bed and stayed there until he died. There wasn't a lot of action in the 600 pages – just a sense that life without love was pointless and without meaning.

Contrast that with the story of Jesus' encounter with a woman who was a 'sinner' – probably a prostitute (Luke 7:36–50). Overwhelmed by the way in which Jesus conveyed God's love and forgiveness, she slipped into a dinner party at which he was a guest. Kneeling at his feet, she poured expensive perfume on him and mixed it with tears of joy. The host was embarrassed at having his party gate-crashed. After all, she belonged on the edge of society and had no business disturbing his respectable home. But Jesus saw her simply as a woman loved and valued by God, and gave her a new future: 'Your faith has saved you; go in peace.'

God's love means that he gives himself to us, accepts us as we are and opens up a new life for us. He doesn't manipulate us or play power games with us. From beyond ourselves he brings a new strength and new possibilities for our lives.

## We're part of God's plan

Hope grows also from a sense of knowing our roots and knowing where we're going. Without that, we're locked into the present. To live for the present moment is exciting for a time. Past and future are remote and irrelevant, we imagine. But constantly living on the highs of present moments gives no shape or meaning to life.

Mr Motivator, the TV fitness expert, still leads weekly exercise sessions in a school hall in north London. 'It keeps me in touch with where I've been,' he says. 'If you remember where you've come from, you don't forget where you are, and then you know exactly where you're going.'

Unless we are aware of our past and our future, we imagine that the present is the only way things can be. That may be fine while things are going well. But when things go badly, it spells disaster. Real hope comes from knowing the past and the future of God's plans. We are secure in the knowledge that God has created us: we aren't just a chance collection of atoms, but people loved by God for whom God has a purpose. We look back to the life, death and resurrection of Jesus. Through him we were given a personal stake in God's plan for the world.

And for the future we are caught up in God's great plan, which is moving towards the climax when he will 'bring all creation together, everything in heaven and on earth, with Christ as head' (Ephesians 1:10, GNB). God won't give up until his way of love has won its victory in the world.

## God is leading us forward

As a child I was lucky with my parents. They created a secure family. If they made promises to us, they kept them. We knew the guidelines within which we were expected to behave. So, in a sense, my parents were predictable. But they were also full of surprises – an unexpected outing, perhaps, or a visitor whom we loved to have staying with us.

God is something like that – faithful, but with surprises up his sleeve. 'Promises, promises!' has today become the cynical response of people weary with the tricks of advertisers and politicians. But God's people have found him to be a faithful promise-keeper. 'Let us hold unswervingly to the hope we profess, for he who promised is faithful,' wrote one author who knew a lot about the story of God's people through 2,000 years (Hebrews 10:23).

But there are surprises as well as faithfulness. God isn't in a rut, simply repeating the same old things like a comedian recycling old jokes. He is always leading us forward into new experiences of his creative love, as he moves his plans towards their climax. So to be a Christian is an adventure. It's like going on a journey where you have a good idea of the destination but you don't know what's round the next corner.

The writer to the Hebrews describes the great heroes of the Old Testament as people living an adventure of faith.

> By faith Abraham, when called to go to a place he would later receive as his inheritance, obeyed and went, even though he did not know where he was going. By faith he made his home in the promised land like a stranger in a foreign country. He lived in tents . . . For he was looking forward to the city with foundations, whose architect and builder is God.
>
> (Hebrews 11:8–10)

When you read the scrapes that people like Abraham got into, you can hardly imagine that serving God is boring. Difficult, dangerous sometimes. But adventurous, because it's about serving a God who is working out his purpose in history and in our own lives. He is, in Paul's words, 'the God of hope' (Romans 15:13).

## Living in hope

We don't know when Jesus' final coming will be. 'It's like a man going away,' said Jesus. 'He leaves servants in charge of his house, each with his tasks to do, and tells the doorkeeper to be on the watch. So keep awake, because you don't know whether the owner will return in the evening or at midnight or in the early hours' (see Mark 13:33–34).

Some people who hear this story think that to prepare for Christ's coming they have to be involved in frantic activity all the time. Or they think it's like standing on tiptoe, straining your eyes to catch the first glimpse of the Lord arriving. But anyone who's stood on tiptoe trying to see over a crowd knows you can't do it for long.

No. Preparing for Christ's coming isn't like standing on tiptoe. In his story Jesus talked about the owner of the house leaving his servants with their tasks to do. That's what it's about – steadily getting on with the tasks entrusted to us and being the kind of people God has called us to be. What will this involve?

## Living in the Spirit

First, we are people of the Spirit. It's God's Spirit who makes us aware of God's love for us and enables us to live in God's strength. But there is more than that. The Spirit, Paul wrote, 'is a deposit guaranteeing our inheritance until the redemption of those who are God's possession' (Ephesians 1:14). The Spirit is God's down-payment of our inheritance, the first instalment of the life of God's coming reign. He gives a foretaste of heaven – only a taste, but a real taste. God has given him to us so that we may demonstrate the life of heaven on earth!

The main mark of the Spirit at work is that he makes us more Christlike. Our hope of meeting Christ at his coming inspires our desire to be like him:

> When he is revealed, we will be like him, for we will see him as he is. And all who have this hope in him purify themselves, just as he is pure. (1 John 3:2–3, NRSV)

As followers of Jesus, we are called to reflect his character. And as we allow his Spirit to work in us, he gets to work on the way we are. He doesn't squash our personality, but chips away at those bits of our character which don't look like Christ, and fills us with the qualities of Christ. Paul says it's like a harvest which God's Spirit produces in us – a harvest of love, joy, peace, patience, kindness, generosity, faithfulness, gentleness and self-control (Galatians 5:23).

But love, which heads the list, is the surest evidence of God's work in us, the toughest demand he can make on us. 'Love' today has many meanings. 'I love chocolate fudge cake.' 'Let's make love.' 'Mummy won't love you unless you behave yourself.' Often when people talk about 'falling in love' they mean 'falling in love with the experience of falling in love'. That has more to do with satisfying my own desire than with giving myself to the other person.

Real love is about self-giving. It's not about pleasing others in order to get something out of them, or using them to satisfy my own needs. It's not so much about feelings as about caring actions towards others. It's often difficult and costly, like Jesus' giving of himself for humanity. Philip Yancey wrote:

> How hard it is to remember that the kingdom of God calls me to love the woman who has just emerged from the abortion clinic (and even her doctor), the promiscuous person who is dying of AIDS, the wealthy landowner who is exploiting God's creation. If I have trouble loving such people, I need to ask if I have understood Jesus' gospel.
>
> (*Christianity Today*, 25 February 1995, p. 104)

### A life of self-giving

Secondly, living in hope means living not for self but for self-giving. We make a lot these days of self-expression and self-fulfilment. We talk about 'loving myself'. Or we say, 'I have a duty to myself.' We are the me-generation. And we look for instant satisfaction of our desires. On the level of material goods, the credit card has 'taken the waiting out of wanting'. The same expectation of instant satisfaction has seeped into every area of life.

Now there is a truth in the desire for self-fulfilment. God doesn't mean us to be negative about ourselves or to go on pointless trips of self-denial just to show what saints we are. But a culture of self-fulfilment is a short-cut to disaster. It makes relationships shallow and it turns individuals in on themselves.

There are Christian versions of it which undermine real hope. People ask themselves, 'What am I getting out of the church's worship now?' 'Why don't I feel that God is doing much for me now?' In some contexts those might be healthy questions. But often they are the cries of people who are living only for the present. They have little sense of moving forward with God towards the completion of his plan for the world.

We are a generation of spectators. On average, we watch thirty hours per week of television. We are learning to prefer virtual reality to the reality of a broken world. Many young people seem wholly detached from the larger world. They are sealed into an electronic world of music, films, video games and MTV.

As they grow up, all the pressures on them are to get a career going, make money and develop their lifestyle. The radical demands of Jesus are heard only very faintly in the background. To hear what he really said comes as a shock:

Those who want to save their lives will lose them, but those who lose their lives for me and for the gospel will save them. What good is it for you to gain the whole world, yet forfeit your soul?
(Mark 8:35-36)

Or, as Steve Turner put it, 'There's more to life than everything.'

Christians, like other people, are concerned to feel good about themselves, to have satisfying spiritual experiences. But the Christian message isn't about feeling good or having spiritual highs. It's an invitation to enter God's kingdom, to submit to his rule, to get involved with his work of remaking the world. Where are the young people who will say these words?

I see that God has goals to achieve in the world.

I see that nothing matters more than to set my mind on God's reign and his justice.

I see that Jesus calls me to give my whole self to his service, whatever demands that may make on me.

I see he promises that in giving myself to that mission I will find my real self.

That's what I want to be involved in. Wherever it takes me, I want to be there.

As far as I know my own heart, I offer myself to his service.

Being an actor rather than a spectator in God's mission involves finding our particular place in God's plan. What is the particular contribution which God has for me in achieving his goals? There are enough different tasks to be done to suit the varieties of gifts which God has given us.

I like to think, for example, of the prophet Elijah when he was battling to defend Israel's faith in the true God, while King Ahab was doing his best to introduce foreign gods and to lead people away from the Lord. Elijah fearlessly played his role as a religious leader, confronting the king despite the risk to his own life. But there was another man of God, Obadiah – a high-ranking official at Ahab's court – who was quietly working to minimize the effect of Ahab's pagan influences. He was risking his life by hiding other prophets of Israel's God to keep them safe from Ahab's secret police (1 Kings 18:3–4).

Both these men played a vital role in God's mission. Neither was doing something more important than the other. Each was doing what his gifts fitted him for and what God had called him to.

In God's mission today, some of us are called to specific roles of service in the church. Others are called to practise Christian values in the world of work and in the community. Some are called to stay in familiar places. Others are called to serve Christ in other cultures. No-one is more important than others. God expects each of us to 'lose our life' for Christ's sake, to see our life as given to his service.

## Knowing where our true wealth is

Thirdly, hope means not clinging to this world's wealth as though it were the only world there is. The Bible describes Abraham and other faithful Israelites as 'strangers and foreigners [or pilgrims] on the earth' because 'they desire a better country, that is, a heavenly one' (Hebrews 11:13–16, NRSV). We are citizens of heaven (Philippians 3:20). That's where we most truly belong, and it affects all our values.

This isn't to say we should all become hermits or hippies. Far from being a recluse, Jesus got a reputation as a party-goer. He knew that this world is God's world, and in it God 'richly provides us with everything for our enjoyment' (1 Timothy 6:17). Yet he also insisted that even if you have more than enough, your possessions don't give you life (Luke 12:15).

In 1793 the Chinese emperor politely refused gifts offered by envoys of King George III, saying that his people had no use for the manufactured goods of his visitors. Before long he was proved entirely wrong. They wanted them, they loved them, and they would try anything to get them. They were like us. We assume that as life goes on, our standard of living should rise. The very way we use the phrase 'standard of living' shows how central money and possessions are to our view of life. But the radical demands of God's reign put a question mark against that assumption.

Few things are more exciting, if we have money at our disposal, than giving it to projects in God's mission and watching them grow. Dietrich Bonhoeffer wrote bluntly: 'Let no-one say, "God has blessed me with money and possessions", and then live as if he and his God were alone in the world.'

## Living through suffering

Fourthly, living in hope means experiencing the pattern of death and resurrection which we see in Jesus. Sometimes we are battered by suffering and there seems no way out. We are 'hoping against hope', clinging on to God's promises without any sense that he is present in the crisis. At other times we feel that, because we have experienced God's faithfulness in the past, our hope for the future can be more confident. 'The one who calls you is faithful and he will do it' (1 Thessalonians 5:24).

Father Jerzy Popieluszko, a Polish priest martyred by the communists in 1984, said: 'A Christian must be a sign of contradiction in the world.' He lived out that contradiction in his fearless criticism of the state's oppression. He constantly urged that violence should be overcome by peace, evil by love. And he knew that even though his resistance might seal his own fate, God has a way of contradicting death with life.

He shared the conviction of Paul, who wrote from his own experience of suffering as an apostle of Christ:

We always carry around in our body the death of Jesus, so that the life of Jesus may also be revealed in our body. For we who are alive are always being given over to death for Jesus' sake, so that his life may be revealed in our mortal body. So then, death is at work in us, but life is at work in you . . . We know that the one who raised the Lord Jesus from the dead will also raise us with Jesus and present us with you in his presence.

(2 Corinthians 4:10–14)

As a missionary in China in the late 1930s, Leslie Lyall found himself in a battle zone between Chinese and Japanese forces. 'For a few days,' he wrote, 'I was in the depths of despondency. And yet, faced with possible evacuation, we were still planting seeds in the Kiangchow garden and the spring blossoms were in bloom. Somehow, there was a strong hope.'

In 1951 he was expelled by the Chinese communist rulers, and the Christians among whom he had worked mostly went underground. But by the time of his death in 1996 he knew of the amazing resurgence of the church in China – a church in which many of the people he had influenced as students had later become leaders. Out of what seemed like death God had brought resurrection.

## Putting prayer first

Finally, living in hope means being committed to prayer. Jesus taught us to pray, 'Your kingdom come, your will be done on earth as it is in heaven' (Matthew 6:10). Prayer isn't the only thing we do for God's reign. But it's the most basic thing we do, because in prayer we are saying to God: 'It's your reign we long for, it's your will that we long to see done. We want to put our will in line with yours. And we're asking you to set loose in the world the power of your reign.'

God expects us to live as subjects of his rule and to co-operate energetically with his work towards bringing in his kingdom in its fullness. But the fact that 'Your kingdom come' is a prayer reminds us constantly that God's reign will come by his act and his generosity, not by human achievement. When we can do nothing else, we can pray.

The first all-race elections were due in South Africa in April 1994. Natal was ravaged by fighting between supporters of the African National Congress and the Inkatha Freedom Party. The state was descending into a whirlpool of violence, and Chief Buthulezi, the leader of Inkatha, was refusing to join in the elections. International mediators tried without success to bring the parties together and went home shattered.

Then suddenly, only six days before the elections were due, Chief Buthulezi changed his mind, 80 million new voting papers were issued, and people of all races queued together to vote for the leaders of a new South Africa.

What is less well known is the story told by Michael Cassidy in *A Witness For Ever*. Behind the scenes there were Christians quietly bringing party leaders together to develop trust. And people all over South Africa and around the world were praying that the crisis would be resolved. When the breakthrough came, newspaper editors produced headlines such as 'How God stepped in to save South Africa'. And the BBC called it 'a miracle and an answer to prayer'.

## Words of encouragement

Hope is focused on the future. But it is lived in the present. It's hard to live as subjects of God's rule in a world which refuses his rule. But there are two promises to keep us going if ever we are discouraged. First, the promise that our service for God is never wasted. After describing the hope of Christ's coming and the resurrection of all God's people, Paul came to his conclusion:

> Therefore, my beloved, be steadfast, immovable, always excelling in the work of the Lord, because you know that in the Lord your labour is not in vain.
>
> (1 Corinthians 15:58, NRSV)

Because at his coming Christ will set up his reign for ever, all that we do in the service of his reign has lasting value.

The second promise is that nothing can separate us from Christ's love – and therefore he stands between us and everything which might undermine our hope:

> Who will separate us from the love of Christ? Will hardship, or distress, or persecution, or famine, or nakedness, or peril, or sword? . . . No, in all these things we are more than conquerors through him who loved us. For I am convinced that neither death, nor life . . . nor anything else in all creation, will be able to separate us from the love of God in Christ Jesus our Lord.      (Romans 8:35–39, NRSV)

# IS THERE A FUTURE FOR THE WORLD?

'Why accept the present when you have the power to change it?' The words in the newspaper were an advert for Microsoft. They were seeking 'talented individuals who share our passion for quality and integrity', ambitious people keen 'to fulfil this vision'.

'If Microsoft is looking for people eager to fulfil its vision,' I thought, 'what about God and his vision? Isn't he intent on changing the world?' Then I realized there was a problem. There are many Christians who see no point in trying to change the world for the better, because they believe it's bound to get worse. That's what prophecy declares, they say.

'Do you realize,' a student remarked to Tom Sine at one of his futures conferences in the United States, 'if we start feeding hungry people, things won't get worse, and if things don't get worse, Jesus won't come?' She'd been taught the fatalistic view of prophecy we looked at in chapter 5, and it made her steer clear of any commitment to social action.

There's another reason many Christians aren't involved in trying to change the world. They've settled for a form of discipleship which sees God as a private experience or a passport to heaven. But if God is really God, he can't be a secret charm hanging round my neck. He's the Creator with a mission to renew the world, and looking for the co-operation of his people.

## No earthly use?

It's a fashionable lie to say that because Christians look for a life beyond death they're no use for dealing with earthly problems. The truth is exactly the opposite. Because we're released by Christ from anxiety about our death, we can give our energy to work for the transformation of this world. 'No man is ready to live life on earth until he is ready for life in heaven,' wrote C. S. Lewis. And he added:

> The Christians who did most for the present world were just those who thought most about the next . . . It is since Christians have largely ceased to think of the other world that they have become so ineffective in this. Aim at heaven and you will get earth 'thrown in': aim at earth and you will get neither.

But still the question persists: what reason is there to believe that we can change the world? Isn't it presumptuous for us to think that we can achieve what only God can do when Christ comes again? Now it's true that only God will bring an end to evil and only God will create the new heavens and the new earth. Language about men and women 'bringing in' God's kingdom is a distortion of the biblical message. But there are reasons to hope that in God's strength the world can be made a better place.

Although God's reign is yet to come in its completeness, it

has already dawned. Its power is at work in the world. Jesus has won the decisive victory over demonic forces which work through the political and social systems of the world. 'Having disarmed the powers and authorities, he made a public spectacle of them, triumphing over them by the cross' (Colossians 2:15).

God doesn't keep the power of his reign locked inside the church. Old Testament prophets saw God at work in the rise and fall of pagan rulers, weaving his plans into the ups and downs of history. Jesus' healings – signs of God's reign in action – weren't confined to the circle of believers, but spilled over into the wider world.

He expects his followers today to reflect the pattern of his ministry – to fight disease, to overcome evil, to set free the oppressed. To settle for less is to turn the good news into fairly good news. It's to tear the plan of God in half.

## The world as we know it

In chapter 1 we surveyed some of the issues in today's world which threaten hope. They aren't merely a rag-bag of unconnected problems. They interact with each other in complex ways which make them difficult to deal with. A quick sketch might look like this.

The development of capitalism and of industry during the last 200 years has led in the western world to increased productivity. This in turn has brought improved standards of living and all the trappings of a consumer society – including the pollution produced by industrial processes and by the burning of fossil fuels for heating and transport.

Among the by-products of this industrial activity are the destruction of the ozone layer and the development of global warming. The melting of polar ice-caps leads to a rise in sea levels – perhaps half a metre over the next 100 years. This will have a devastating effect on low-lying land from Bangladesh to Hamburg. And weather patterns are becoming more and more extreme, making food production more uncertain.

Meanwhile, population pressures and the desire for economic growth cause the destruction of tropical rainforests. The forests are thus less able to perform one of their roles – absorbing carbon dioxide and converting it into oxygen. So the greenhouse-gas problem is made worse. And both people and animals whose home is in the forests are threatened with extinction.

The world's relentlessly growing population requires ever greater food production. The serious decline of fish stocks in many parts of the world results from that need, compounded by ruthless competition in the fishing industry. And the dumping of industrial waste in the seas is causing genetic disorders and infertility in some fish.

The prophet Hosea sensed the connection between human conflict and the devastation of the earth:

> There is no faithfulness or loyalty,
>    and no knowledge of God in the land.
> Swearing, lying, and murder,
>    and stealing and adultery break out;
>    bloodshed follows bloodshed.
> Therefore the land mourns,
>    and all who live in it languish.
> Together with the wild animals
>    and the birds of the air,
>    even the fish of the sea are perishing.
>                                    (Hosea 4:1–3, NRSV)

The population increase may not be the main problem. Even more damaging is the way in which people use the earth's resources. A baby born in the West will use thirty-four times the resources of a baby born in Bangladesh. And it's Europe, not Africa or Asia, which is the world's most thickly populated continent.

This brings us back to the so-called developed world, where consumerism is rapidly producing a plastic world. Humanity, which once stood in awe at the power of nature, has conquered it and throttled it and covered it with tarmac and empty Coke cans. All this in the name of an economic system we call the free market.

But what brings a kind of freedom to some keeps others in bondage to poverty and lack of choice. During the last 500 years, western wealth was boosted by colonization, the slave trade and exploitation of the resources of Africa and South America.

And now we have an interest in keeping the system the way it is. Only 15% of the world's population enjoys our standard of living. Clearly the earth couldn't supply the resources or absorb the pollution if the whole population were to live at this level. So we put up trade barriers, we keep out asylum-seekers. We ensure that the crippling debt of poor countries prevents their making progress.

This creates a world which is essentially unstable, making armed conflict between nations, and civil unrest within nations, a constant possibility. Within both western and Two-Thirds World countries the gap between rich and poor people is growing. Beside me is a photo showing a huge advertiser's hoarding with the caption: 'Take a trip to luxury-land on a Vono executive bed.' Sheltering beneath it are fifteen homeless people. The photo comes from Nigeria, but it could easily be London or Washington.

If there are nations which have no real stake in the world economy, there are people in every nation who have no real stake in society. They may be unemployed, or unlucky, or unloved, or caught up from childhood in a culture of drugs and violence. For a host of complex reasons they feel abandoned, unvalued, without hope. They are the victims of a society which rushes on without them. Progress always has its price. For, as someone has said,

> If we idolize wealth, we create poverty.
> If we idolize success, we create the inadequate.
> If we idolize power, we create powerlessness.

## A different dream

For all its benefits, the western dream of economic progress is flawed. We need to look again at another dream, as Nigerian author Ben Okri urges:

> As the millennium draws to a close . . . this is precisely the time to dream the best dream of them all: that no peoples will know starvation, that no nation will be oppressed by another, that tyranny will not be able to exist unpunished, that liberty be given a more glorious song.

But *why* dream this particular dream? One of the ironies of today's world is that we've thrown away the idea that there are any absolute values. Everyone makes up his or her own values. There's no overriding truth by which all things are judged. The truth is simply 'what's true for me'. And yet we *need* common values if we are to turn the world from its flight towards self-destruction. We need to look again at the values of the creator God and his plan for the world's renewal.

In chapter 3 we summarized the vision of the Hebrew prophets of God's goals for the world:

- to create a community of people from all nations who would live under his just and gentle rule;
- to banish the evil inside and around us, which constantly makes human life less than it was meant to be;
- to create a world of justice where the poor are oppressed no longer;
- to build a world of peace between nations;
- to bring men and women into harmony rather than conflict with the natural world;
- to create a permanent celebration of life as all God's people experience the closeness of relationship to the living God.

That's what God will do when his reign comes in its completeness. That's what is meant by his bringing 'all creation together, everything in heaven and on earth, with Christ as head' (Ephesians 1:10). And if that's what the King will ultimately achieve in the future, it shapes the goals and values of those who are subjects of the King now.

## Living the dream

Nelson Mandela had been in gaol for twelve of his twenty-seven years of imprisonment when he received a visit from his daughter and her newborn baby. It's the custom among his people for a grandfather to name his grandchild, and the baby girl had come to be named. The name he chose was Zaziwe – which means 'hope'.

'The name had a special meaning for me,' he wrote later, 'for during all my years in prison hope never left me – and now it never would. I was convinced that this child would be a part of a new generation of South Africans for whom apartheid would be a distant memory – that was my dream.'

As he held that fragile child, he dreamed the future. In the act of naming her he gave concrete expression to his hope. Our vision, our dream, of God's reign determines our action now. Let's explore how that dream might shape our hopes for today's world.

## A dream for the universe

First, God's reign will be universal. It will affect all nations. Therefore our concerns can never be merely for 'my group' or 'my nation'. God has no favourites, and we should reflect his character and his concerns.

There was a minor political storm when a British Labour MP was moved from her post as Shadow Transport Minister to that of Shadow Minister of Overseas Development. 'Demoted to Overseas Development' was the phrase used by all the newspapers. It was a sad commentary on the importance which the media – and the politicians? – attach to these matters. We live in a world where one person in five lives in absolute poverty, where 800 million go hungry every night, and where 35,000 children die every day from preventable diseases. If we are to reflect the universal scope of God's love, we need to press for a more serious commitment to issues of world development.

## A dream of community

Secondly, God's reign will create community. Therefore the nurturing of human community is our goal now. This means that we'll look for human solutions to the problems we face, rather than merely economic ones. In the modern city, community has broken down. The scale of things is too huge for people to feel that they belong. People live close to each other without ever knowing each other. A man was found dead in a high-rise flat, with a suicide note beside him: 'Nobody came.'

Many unemployed young people feel abandoned by society, cut adrift without a lifeline. After car accidents and cancer, suicide is the third major cause of death among young people. Youth clubs are closed because government funds are cut. So often nobody listens, nobody asks about the background of people who take out their anger in violence, nobody is there to say, 'You matter to us. Without you our society is in fragments.' God needs people out there on the front line standing with young people, and he needs others in the churches who'll support them when it's tough.

For many people in South American *favelas*, the 'base Christian communities' are a source of hope. Poor people come together to pray and study the Bible, to improve their conditions and to resist police repression. What they can't do individually they find strength to do together. And people in other parts of the world are learning from their experience.

On the global level, we can't express community in the sense of encouraging good personal relationships. But we can say that community between nations is expressed through peace and justice.

### *A dream of peace*

The third point, then, is that God's reign will bring peace. Therefore promoting and maintaining peace is our goal now. Arms sales make an enormous contribution to many western economies. We raise our own standard of living at the cost of encouraging instability and oppression elsewhere.

The most bizarre aspect of the Gulf War in 1991 was that most of the nations who fought against Iraq had helped to build up Iraq's forces. France, Britain, Italy, the United States and West Germany all sold arms to Iraq, and West German businesses helped Saddam Hussein build his notorious chemical warfare plants. The USSR provided 47% of

Baghdad's military supplies. Much of the money for Iraq's purchases came from other oil-producing nations – notably Kuwait and Saudi Arabia.

In July 1996, three women went on trial for breaking into a British Aerospace factory and causing damage amounting to £1.5 million to a Hawk fighter jet. The plane was destined for Indonesia. There was good evidence to show that, like other Hawks sold previously, it would be used against the people of East Timor. This territory was forcibly annexed by Indonesia in 1975, since when – according to Amnesty International – almost 200,000 East Timorese have been killed.

The women, members of a Christian peace group, were acquitted on the grounds that they were using reasonable force to prevent a much greater crime. Their methods may be controversial, but they showed that it's possible for ordinary people to do something to challenge the cynical supply of killing machines for the sake of profit.

A question Christians should often ask is: 'What shall I do, because of what Christ has done?' If Christ came into the world to make peace between humanity and God and to break down barriers of hostility between people, we are called to be peacemakers. We may do that personally among the people where we live and work. On the broader front, we may speak for peace and resist the equipping of nations for war.

## A dream of justice

Fourthly, God's reign will bring justice. Therefore justice is our goal. 'Seek first the reign of God and his justice,' said Jesus. 'Blessed are those who hunger and thirst for justice, for they will be filled' (Matthew 6:33; 5:6, my translation). Justice in the Bible isn't the impartial dispensing of verdicts in the lawcourt. It involves acting to put right what is wrong, delivering the victims of injustice.

In this sense, justice involves trying to narrow the huge gaps between rich and poor. The gap between rich and poor in Britain is bigger than at any time since the 1880s. And the world's poorer nations are crippled by the debt they owe to the wealthy. We should add our voice to those calling for the cancelling of the debt of the poorest countries.

Another kind of injustice is the exploitation of cheap labour. You might spend £50 on a pair of trainers. But the forty factory workers in the Philippines who helped to make them share in just over £1 of that price between them. The rest goes in profit, transport, advertising and sponsorship deals. Working conditions in the factories leave much to be desired. Your favourite football team may get millions just for wearing and advertising the product. Maybe through the supporters' club you could urge the management to raise the matter with the manufacturers?

Justice is about a host of other issues: adequate support for the disabled, for example, or nursery education for children who've had a bad start in life, or homes for the homeless. People who hunger and thirst for justice will seek such issues out and see how change can happen.

An ancient Greek philosopher was asked, 'When will justice come?' He replied, 'Justice will come when those of us who are not injured are as outraged as those who are.' Where can thoughtful, compassionate Christian outrage be found?

### A dream of harmony with nature

Fifthly, God's reign will involve bringing humanity and the natural world into harmony. Therefore we are to care for the environment now. The world isn't a disposable asset to be replaced, when Christ comes, with something entirely different. It is to be cared for as something good which God has made and will transform.

This means (to use the jargon) that we must promote 'sustainable development'. In other words, we must

- seek change for the better at a rate which can benefit people of all countries, not simply those who are already rich;
- use natural resources at a rate which doesn't ignore the needs of future generations;
- limit pollution and greenhouse-gas emissions to levels which the earth can actually absorb – and that means substantial reductions by western countries in order to allow some room for development by Two-Thirds World countries;
- protect the natural environment from destructive exploitation of plant life and of human and animal habitats.

The danger is that everyone expects someone else to act on these issues. Governments are reluctant to take tough and radical action because they don't think other governments will follow suit, and because they're terrified of being unpopular with voters if they limit car use or increase the price of petrol substantially. Individuals won't take action, arguing, 'Why should I limit my freedom when the next person isn't prepared to?'

Meanwhile the planet coughs its way to terminal illness. We need visionaries who will argue the case for radical change. We need people who are prepared – together – to set an example and to press for more government action. After all, there are far more people belonging to the various green pressure groups in Britain than to all the political parties put together. And the same is true in many other countries.

# Time for a change

Change will be painful. But the only alternative to change is to bequeath our children a junk yard, in which 85% of the world's people are still poor, still in debt, still wondering what kind of human beings the rest of us are. We look back on our Christian ancestors and wonder why it took till the nineteenth century to get rid of the slave trade. Will future generations look back at us and wonder why we were so slow to get tough with poverty and the rape of the planet?

If we took the kind of steps which have to be taken, we might be in for a pleasant surprise. We might find that less car use brings better health. We might find that being less obsessed with being 'consumers', we have more time to enjoy our friends. We might find that enjoying closer harmony with the created world makes it easier to be in harmony with the Creator.

We are surrounded by huge problems, confronted each day with new examples of injustice and human evil. What hope is there of change? What can ordinary people do? A lot. The peaceful revolution in East Germany in 1989 came out of peace prayer groups in Leipzig. Little groups of five or ten people had been meeting for years, gradually growing until the movement became unstoppable and the Berlin Wall fell down.

Nelson Mandela, addressing his first rally in Soweto after his release from prison in 1990, said, 'I am more convinced than ever before, it is not kings and generals that change history. It is the masses of the people.'

## Little people, big vision

Change happens when little people have a big vision. Robert Kennedy described his brother President John F. Kennedy:

'Some men see things as they are and say "Why?" But he dreams things that never were and says "Why not?"' We believe in God who 'gives life to the dead and calls into existence the things that do not exist' (Romans 4:17, NRSV). He has given us a vision of a different kind of world and invites us to say, 'Why not?'

No one person can take on all these issues, plus the scores of others I might have mentioned. But it's realistic to take one one or two such issues and

- understand them;
- keep up to date by joining an appropriate charitable or campaigning organization;
- give regularly to such organizations;
- inform others about the issue and support them as they find their own ways of practising justice and peace;
- take action locally;
- aim to live as a 'global citizen' by thinking ethically about things you buy – for example, by being willing to pay more for fairly traded coffee and refusing to buy timber which hasn't come from managed forests; and by setting personal targets for actions such as reducing car use and recycling.

Often we feel that our contribution can make no difference, like digging the Channel Tunnel with a penknife. But everything we do, however insignificant, to build community, justice and love is an act of faith and hope in the God who will make everything new. The world isn't changed by naïve optimism, but by stubborn perseverance in response to a vision, and by God who never gives up on his plan to mend a broken world.

# A CHURCH FACING FORWARDS

'Facing the direction of travel, sir, or facing backwards?' Once I'd come to terms with his complicated way of asking the question, I gave the man on the phone the answer that most people give. I wanted my reserved seat on the train to face forwards.

Although, if you're in a crash, it's safer in a train or plane to face backwards, most of us prefer to look where we're going. Yet in the church we seem to prefer looking backwards. Styles of worship, patterns of church government, times of services and many other things carry the baggage of times past. To many people, especially the young, 'church' means a boring, irrelevant institution. A switch-off.

## Celebrate the past

Don't misunderstand me. I'm not one for throwing something away just because it's old. And I've argued in this book that our past is important. If we have no memory, we don't know who we are, and so we can't find meaning for the future.

The first task of the church is to celebrate what God has done in the past, because there we find the clue to his plans for the world and for our own lives. In particular, the story of Israel and the life, death and resurrection of Jesus tell us that the community of faith is formed by God's own generosity. The church may sometimes lose sight of its grounding in the extravagant love which created it, but God himself never does.

So the past is fundamental to the church's well-being. But remembering the past is one thing; living in it is another thing altogether. People are looking for meaning in their lives; they are open to possible answers. But they don't know where to turn. And mostly they don't even imagine that the church might be a place to find answers.

Douglas Coupland, whose novel *Life After God* I mentioned in chapter 2, doesn't cynically reject Christianity. He discards it almost wistfully, feeling he is 'cut off' from Christian beliefs 'in a way that was never connectable'. So in the novel he doesn't end up on his knees in church, but finds himself naked in an ancient forest. Churches which don't learn to respond to this searching will find themselves in terminal decline.

But this search for meaning is our opportunity. The Princeton Religion Research Center headlined its 1996 Report: 'Will the vitality of the church be the surprise of the twenty-first century?' The answer to that question will be determined largely by whether the churches can learn to face forwards rather than backwards. How can we live as a community of hope?

In this final chapter I want to explore what the features of a forward-facing church might be. I'm not trying to describe *all* the features which might be desirable in a church, but only those which arise from the theme of this book. We begin with some of the images by which the New Testament describes the church.

# Pictures of the church

*A pilgrim people*

The church is a pilgrim people. Not only individual Christians but churches – both nationally and locally – are pilgrims on a journey towards God's future (Hebrews 11). We dare not allow it to be an unchanging institution with vested interests and fossilized structures.

With the impertinence of youth I once suggested to a group of ecumenical dignitaries that there would be no bishops or hierarchies in heaven, but only people whom God loves. So, I went on, might it not be as well to drop some of the baggage of the past and find more flexible ways of being the church? I didn't get a reply, but I still believe what I said.

People distrust unwieldy institutions. What they increasingly feel about politics, royalty, the legal system and all big bureaucracies they feel also about traditional churches. Every church should ask itself: which aspects of our life and organization have passed their sell-by date? Where is our journey forward taking us now?

*A body*

The church is the body of Christ. This is an image of community. It speaks of church as a place to belong. In an age when the internet makes communication impersonal and reality is virtual rather than real, people are hungry for human relationships.

In a church which takes this seriously, individual members will be valued for who they are rather than for how much they earn. Everyone's gifts and contributions will be welcomed. No-one will be too young, too old, too poor, too rich, too clever, too simple, too black, too white, to be a vital part of the community.

They will live with the tensions of expressing both unity and variety, because they know that both are true to the gospel. To bring people together in unity is God's great goal for the world. But to give space to individual personalities and gifts is to value the uniqueness of each member, instead of pressurizing them into conformity.

Maybe the trickiest aspect of that tension concerns patterns of worship. People have differing needs and preferences – all-age worship, choral evensong, charismatic freedom, Taizé, the use of visual symbols, focus on preaching, big celebration, small fellowship group . . . the list is endless. Do you mix some of these things up in a single service? Or have services of different types? Or say that your church can do only one style well, and you'll stick to that, leaving room for other churches to offer different styles?

No solution is straightforward. No church can give up on the conviction that 'there is neither Jew nor Greek, slave nor free, male nor female, for you are all one in Christ Jesus' (Galatians 3:28). To be true to the Christian vision, we have to be committed to holding such varieties together. And yet a church may struggle to respond to the needs of all. Each church must weigh up what it will try to achieve. But if it simply ignores the tension – for example, by opting to cater for the needs of a narrow group – it is not being faithful to its calling.

People will take responsibility for each other, rather than relying on paid officials to work on their behalf. Two of the most significant words in their Bibles will be 'each other'. They will pray for each other, forgive each other, teach and learn from each other, encourage each other, bear each other's burdens. They will know the words of Jesus, 'Love each other as I have loved you' (John 15:12). They will know how hard it is to live like this, but they will know the depth of human well-being which comes from it. They will be anticipating the life of heaven, as Oscar, a Nicaraguan peasant, suggests:

> There's no point in talking about heaven, wanting now to go up to heaven to see what kind of place it is; I think we've got enough on our hands to see what kind of a place the earth is . . . When people love each other there's a community of love, and that's heaven: where there's no divisions, no selfishness, where there's no deceit, that's where heaven is, that *is* heaven, that's glory.  (C. Rowland, *Revelation*, Epworth, 1993, p. 47)

Usually, when the New Testament pictures the church as the body of Christ, it is speaking of the local church. But in Colossians and Ephesians Paul applies it to the whole church. This reminds us that local churches are not private islands, but belong together as Christian brothers and sisters.

A church which takes this seriously will have links with another church or churches. For instance, a suburban church will form a partnership with an inner-city church so that they may learn from each other's experience and support each other in practical ways. And it will form links across the world, for example with a church in another continent. To have links with an overseas *church* is quite different from supporting a *missionary* working overseas. It's a relationship of equality and mutual enrichment.

### A witness to God's reign

The church is a colony of heaven (Philippians 3:20). Paul was writing to the church at Philippi, a colony of Rome. It was the role of a Roman colony to be a kind of small-scale copy of Rome and to represent it in the region where it was set. The church is called to live by the values of heaven – love, peace, justice – and so demonstrate to the world the reality of God and the values of his reign.

James describes the church as 'a kind of first fruits of his creatures' (James 1:18, NRSV). The firstfruits were the beginning of the harvest, a promise that the rest of the harvest was to follow. So to describe the church in this way means that the church embodies now what is God's purpose for all.

Another way to put this is to say that the church is a witness and a servant of God's reign. We saw the scope of God's reign in chapter 3, and in chapter 11 we explored how that vision may shape our action in society. Here I want to underline how the vision affects the church as a community, rather than simply a collection of individuals.

It means that the church's mission to people in its locality isn't merely to bring people into personal commitment to Jesus, nor merely to offer service to the local community. It's to announce the lordship of Christ over both individuals and society, to seek the world's healing as well as individual salvation.

Carl-Erik Sahlberg is minister of a church in central Stockholm. When he arrived, there was a congregation of three. Over seven years the numbers swelled to 300. The work was very tough because in the area around the church there is widespread drug addiction, prostitution and a host of social problems.

But they opened the church every day, as if to say, 'We are here for you.' Others began to share in the ministry. They found a house where they could offer food and friendship. They spent time on the streets. They prayed for two hours in the church each day. The drug abusers and the prostitutes know that there is a church which cares about them. And some of them have become committed to Christ and have changed their lifestyle.

The church's ministry of witnessing to God's reign is a *whole* ministry. We aren't free to choose which bits we prefer. Because God's reign is potentially for all people, we are to be open to all. Groucho Marx wrote to his club: 'Please accept my resignation. I don't want to belong to any club that will accept me as a member.' Those who reflect the intentions of Jesus can't be so choosy. We are to hold out the invitation of his love to every kind of person.

That means especially being alongside those who suffer or are on the underside of society. In his book *The Isaiah Vision*, Raymond Fung tells the story of Mary, a homeless woman in Wichita, Kansas. She was ill with both physical and mental problems, and had turned for help to Venture House, a church project reaching out to the city's down and outs. One day she asked shyly for someone to pray for her.

'Mary, why don't you come early tomorrow and pray with us?' the volunteer suggested. Next day was an overcast Good Friday morning. She sat watching them pray and listened to the reading of the story of Jesus' crucifixion. Thoughtful silence followed, until Mary broke it by saying, 'You know, if there are people like you in the world, perhaps Jesus really was raised from the dead.'

People like Mary can often sense that Jesus – who died at the hands of the powerful – understands what it's like to suffer and not to be understood. He knows their situation and he's on their side. But they will grasp it only if they see it portrayed in the lives of Christians who come close to them.

And that's true of all our witness to God's reign. The most important thing about 'being church' isn't what happens in a church building on Sunday. It's what happens in the lives of God's people the rest of the week. Church leaders tend to measure success by how many people are gathered together on Sunday. That, after all, justifies their existence and their salaries. But the church's mission is mainly what happens when ordinary Christians get involved with their friends and the issues raised at work, in the home and at leisure. And the purpose of Sunday is to celebrate the God who sends people into those situations and equip them to be there with confidence.

That may require a radical change in how the church programme is structured. The 1991 *National Church Life Survey* in Australia found that in a typical week 61% of church members had spoken for a quarter of an hour or longer with only five non-churchgoers or fewer. Only 27% were involved with any club or any community service group not connected with a church. The situation is probably similar in Britain.

One step forward which some churches have adopted is to stop all church meetings in the fourth week of the month, to give members more time to meet other people. And when the church meets for study and worship, there is space for people to share stories of what God is doing in their neighbourhoods, at work and among their friends. There is time to encourage, support and pray for each other, so that all are excited by the sense that together they are witnessing to Christ's lordship over all.

## A proclaiming people

Another description of the church ties it very closely with pre-Christian Israel:

> You are a chosen race, a royal priesthood, a holy nation, God's own people, in order that you may proclaim the mighty acts of him who called you out of darkness into his marvellous light. (1 Peter 2:9, NRSV)

*We've been brought from darkness to light, and we want to shout about it!* The passage doesn't make clear whether this 'proclaiming' is addressed to God in worship or to other people in witness. Maybe both. Certainly a church which is conscious of living in God's light will want to give priority to sharing faith with others. It's natural for a church to want to grow. That's part of the onward movement of God, whose love embraces people 'from every tribe and language and people and nation' (Revelation 5:9, NRSV).

Worship too points to the reality of God's new world. It pierces the barrier between earth and heaven and lifts us into the presence of God. This is what the writer to the Hebrews meant when he wrote:

> You have come . . . to the city of the living God, the heavenly Jerusalem, and to innumerable angels in festal gathering, and to the assembly of the firstborn who are enrolled in heaven, and to God the judge of all, and to the spirits of the righteous made perfect, and to Jesus . . .   (Hebrews 12:22–24, NRSV)

In worship we open our hearts and minds to God in love and praise. And it affects us too. In his play *Equus*, Peter Shaffer writes, 'Without worship you shrink. It's as simple as that.' A rich experience of worship enables people to focus on God and his purpose for the world and for our lives. It keeps us from being manipulated by the false gods which try continually to take over our lives.

## The forward-facing church

A church facing forwards will be responsive to different cultures. It will not get locked into a particular culture when the world has moved on. I recently met a woman who told me she wasn't keen on 'these new songs by Sankey', and wanted to stay with the familiar ones. Since Sankey's songs were no longer exactly at their height of popularity (he died in 1908!), she had a bit of catching up to do.

Being responsive to today's culture will involve giving a reason for the hope that we have (1 Peter 3:15) in a way which tackles today's questions, not yesterday's. Today's questions are about truth – how can we know that anything is true apart from what we feel? They are about community – how can we restore and maintain relationships? They are about the future of our planet – how can we live in harmony with nature rather than destroy it? And about meaning – who am I? What does it mean to be human? How can I find hope in a broken world?

A church sensitive to these issues will have groups where people can explore them with permission not to come up with the 'right' answer. It will have worship which touches not only the mind, but the heart and the senses through music and visual images.

It recognizes that many people come into the church because of a felt need, and the sense that the church has a 'product' which can meet that need. It may be the need to belong, or the search for a spiritual experience to lift them beyond material existence. The sensitive church responds to those needs, but resists the temptation to become a supermarket church selling goods to consumers.

It knows that beneath these felt needs is the need to encounter the living God in all his accepting and demanding love. A workbook used by many in the New Age movement urges readers to repeat, 'My salvation comes from me. It cannot come from anywhere else'. The Christian message is the story of God who comes to bring help from outside ourselves, to remake us as his sons and daughters, to involve us in his renewal of the world.

Of course, what I refer to here as 'today's culture' is only one of many cultures. Churches working with older people, or with people from a Hindu or Muslim background, or many other groups, will encounter different issues. But the point is the same: a forward-facing church will be responsive to the cultures it encounters. It won't try to attract people and relate to them in the same ways as thirty years ago.

The surest test of a church's direction is how it relates to young people. In the 1990s only half of Anglican churches in England have any children's work. Only one in five has any youth work. Many churches which do have young people spend their time waiting for them to become adult Christians, and worrying just a little when many of them don't.

Maybe our priorities would be shaken if we took seriously the fact that Jesus put things the other way round. He wanted adults to become more childlike. 'Unless you change and become like little children, you will never enter the kingdom of heaven' (Matthew 18:3).

Does your church listen to its young people? Does it give them space to worship in the participatory way which many of them welcome? Does it encourage them to take some responsibility for worship and learning in which they are involved? Does it commit a significant part of its budget to work among young people? If the answer to such questions is no, the church is seriously backward-facing.

A forward-facing church will set goals for its work with young people and for the rest of its activities. It knows that without goals it will just drift. Aim at nothing and you're sure to hit it.

I remember a student doing a project on how parishes set goals for their work. He asked some vicars to answer a questionnaire. One which came back included the following:

| *Question:* | What is your vision for your church for the next five years? |
| *Answer:* | I have none. |
| *Question:* | Does your congregation share this vision? |
| *Answer:* | Yes. |

It's easy to be cynical. It's easy to feel that real growth and development are beyond our reach. And of course many churches don't have the resources to take on board more than one or two of the issues mentioned here. But, for people touched by God's Spirit and called to be servants of his reign, defeatism is never an option.

## Tomorrow people

The first Christians were 'tomorrow people'. They lived in a world dominated by a hostile culture and confused in a turmoil of conflicting lifestyles and ideas. But they were convinced that the deepest truth about God and the universe was to be found in a crucified man. They were filled with the Spirit of Christ crucified and risen. Against all odds, they changed the face of history by the power of love and the vision of God's coming reign.

Pierre Teilhard de Chardin once said that 'the world belongs to those who offer it hope'. The world is waiting.

# BOOKS AND RESOURCES

Much of the illustrative material in this book is drawn from newspapers, magazines, broadcasts, reports, books and friends too numerous to mention. Books which have influenced my perspectives or have provided significant amounts of resource information, and which I recommend for further study, include the following:

R. Chandler, *Doomsday* (Word, 1993)

P. Cotterell, *Is God Helpless?* (SPCK, 1996)

R. T. France, *Jesus the Radical* (IVP, 1989)

A. A. Hoekema, *The Bible and the Future* (Paternoster, 1978)

G. E. Ladd, *The Presence of the Future* (SPCK, 1980)

C. M. Pate and C. P. Haines, *Doomsday Delusions* (IVP [USA], 1995)

T. Sine, *Wild Hope* (Monarch, 1992)

J. Wallis, *The Soul of Politics* (Fount, 1994)

B. Witherington, *Jesus, Paul and the End of the World* (IVP [USA], 1992)

N. T. Wright, *The Lord and his Prayer* (SPCK, 1996)